YOU Are the
Value

- Define Your Worth
- Differentiate Your CPA Firm
- Own Your Market

By Leo J. Pusateri

Sponsored by **Private Companies Practice Section (PCPS)**

Notice to Readers

You Are the Value: Define Your Worth, Differentiate Your CPA Firm, Own Your Market does not represent an official position of the American Institute of Certified Public Accountants, and it is distributed with the understanding that the author and publisher are not rendering legal, accounting, or other professional services in the publication. If legal advice or other expert assistance is required, the services of a competent professional should be sought.

Contents

Chapter 7—Who Have You Done It For? 77

Chapter 8—What Makes You Different? 93

Chapter 9—Why Should I Do Business With You? (Real Value) 111

Chapter 13: Competing on Value Begins with a Strategy 161

Chapter 14—What Are You Going to Act On? 171

Acknowledgements

Jim Metzler, vice president of Small Firm Interests for the AICPA, called me one day in 2008 and asked for permission to use my intellectual property for a couple of upcoming AICPA meetings. Jim and I both live in the beautiful Buffalo area, reside in the same suburb, and know each other from crossing paths earlier in our careers, but we never connected professionally until Jim ordered a copy of my first book, *mirror mirror on the wall am i the most valued of them all?—The Ultimate Element of Differentiation is YOU*. This sharing of intellectual property led to a keynote presentation at a 2009 AICPA event and the introduction of my work to members of the AICPA PCPS Executive Committee. Now, here we are with the launch of this. Thank you, Jim, for the confidence you have in my work and, more important, your valued friendship.

I was thrilled to hear that the AICPA also would bring Anita Dennis into my life. Anita's knowledge of the accounting profession is amazing. She has been my writing coach and accounting profession subject matter expert from day one of this project. Thank you, Anita, for keeping me on track and providing a guiding light throughout this project.

Special thanks to Mark Koziel, Amy Stainken, and Natasha Schamberger from the AICPA and Jeff Liebel from my team, who figured out how to make this project work.

And thank you to all my friends from the accounting profession who shared their expertise and perspectives and graciously gave me their time as I worked on this book—Bob Daugherty, Bob Glaser, Dennis Castiglia, Rocco Surace, and Marty Lougen.

To Steve Berman, my own CPA and trusted advisor for many years: you are always there for me. Thank you.

Giles Kavanagh and Brent Wagner, other Pusateri team members, always challenged me with their thinking. Sue Peace and Nicole Wickings were always there to help with typing and communication with Anita.

To all my clients who I have had the pleasure and privilege to work with for many years: we have professionally challenged you and you have challenged us to develop new tools and add applications that take this model of introspection to new levels. Thank you.

Lastly, thank you Ann, my wife and soulmate. Your support has always been truly amazing.

About the Author

Leo Pusateri, President, CEO, Pusateri Consulting and Training

Passionate, inspirational, and motivating are words many would use to describe Leo Pusateri. Affectionately known as the "value man" in the financial services industry, he is also recognized as the industry's premier thought partner of value-based training, not only by senior leaders in the C-suites, but among top advisors as well.

While his core Unique Value Proposition™ remains focused on helping organizations and individuals discover, articulate, and capitalize on their value, Leo's curriculum goes significantly deeper by teaching professionals the principles of reputational value, as well as how to develop and present it. He guides senior leaders who are looking to drive an eight- to nine-figure lift to their businesses. He also leads financial entrepreneurs who are attempting to elevate their stature from "good-to-great" to ultimately become extraordinary in competing on value.

When it comes to knowing, pricing, selling, and "living" your value, Leo's time-honored and proprietary programs are in place around the world. This is a credible testament to his knowledge capital that he enthusiastically shares with clients. He has traveled the globe from Singapore to Spain, from Vancouver to Zurich, New York City to London, and from beautiful Buffalo to San Francisco-among other spots in and outside of the U.S. His travels find him working with senior leadership teams to financial entrepreneurs, representing broker-dealers, RIAs, investment management firms, private banks, family offices, insurance companies and others. Through Leo's robust training programs with clients around the globe, firms have endorsed Leo's skill set as the absolute best-in-class in bringing value-based training to the table.

Due to increased growth, popularity, and utilization of his work throughout North America, Leo opened an office in Toronto and launched Pusateri Canada to extend the intellectual properties and consulting capabilities of his firm. Additionally, in 2008, Pusateri formalized a strategic partnership with PriceMetrix of Toronto, which focuses exclusively on helping financial advisors become better "CEOs" of their business. PriceMetrix customers typically realize increases in assets, revenue and fee-based advisory business. Their programs proactively identify client, product and pricing opportunities.

Leo practices what he preaches and is an authentic role model for consultative, respectful dialogue. He truly lives his values—effortlessly and with undeniable passion—and teaches others what he has learned over his professional lifetime. His highly acclaimed book published in 2002, *mirror mirror on the wall am i the most valued of them all?—The Ultimate Element of Differentiation is YOU*, describes in detail his proprietary and powerful Value Ladder™ process, and continues to be requested by senior executives, managers and advisors alike. In addition to understanding the nuances and the challenges that financial entrepreneurs face in winning mandates from the HNW and UHNW, he also knows the challenges faced by centers of influence and allied professionals. As a result, the American Institute of Certified Public Accountants (AICPA), the governing body of the accounting industry in the U.S., has recognized Leo's work to be the peak of effectiveness and the highest standard of quality in the business. The AICPA contracted with Leo for the development of this book, an e-learning curriculum, and major speaking engagements for their industry.

Horsesmouth.com, an online industry provider of business development strategies, content, and conferences for advisors, touted Leo as best in class for his philosophies on competing on value. He is widely quoted in numerous industry publications and was a popular columnist for Financial Advisor magazine. Earlier in his distinguished career, Leo led the sales and marketing efforts for a nationally recognized investment advisory firm, and consulted with Fortune 500 companies, concentrating on sales productivity issues. His experience of more than 30 years, coupled with a keen understanding of successfully working with high net worth clients and his work in the training and the behavior change world, have catapulted Leo into the highest sphere of understanding the intricacies of marketing and positioning financial services with the utmost confidence, passion and speed. In addition, he strives to eliminate what Leo describes as the number one disease in the financial services industry: winging it.

Whether it is distinguishing a firm by driving key economic metrics such as net new assets and price realization, or teaching a large team of financial advisors how to know, price, sell, and live their value, Leo not only forges strategic partnerships, but also—and more importantly—as he is known to say, "lifetime friendships."

Leo is a 1977 graduate of St. Bonaventure University with a BBA degree in Marketing. He is a past alumni board member and is currently serving on the Business Advisory Board to the Dean of the Business School. Currently an active member of the Country Club of Buffalo, Leo has served on various committees to assist the club in achieving its goals.

What Leo cherishes most is his family and friends. Happily residing (as he describes it) in "beautiful Buffalo," he is a devoted husband of 31 years, loving father of four, and proud to say that his eldest daughter is working in the financial services industry. His other three children are pursuing their passions with Leo and his wife's guidance. In the past, he has spent many years, including two as president, on his children's school board at St. Gregory the Great. Leo is not only a coach in the financial services industry, but with his limited spare time, he is also coaching his son for his Sunday night Youth Basketball League. Even he can't put a value on that.

Foreword

By James C. Metzler, CPA
Vice President, Small Firm Interests, AICPA

As I write this, we are taking the first steps out of a worldwide recession that has shaken all sectors of the economy, from the largest banks to the smallest businesses. The clients that CPAs serve are experiencing shrinking demand for their goods and services, disappearing credit lines, large layoffs, and severely restricted cash flow. As a result, business owners and families are scrutinizing every expense. They are reevaluating their relationships with their CPA firms and the fees they pay them.

Sound familiar? As someone who practiced in a local firm for 32 years, I have experienced more business down cycles than I care to remember. I can't help but reflect on my years in public practice and the challenges we are facing today. What has enabled so many firms to survive and even thrive in tough times? What is it about a firm that makes its clients stick with it even when the competition offers a dramatically lower fee quote? And, once you identify this special quality, how do you use it to your firm's advantage?

I spent my entire public practice career in "beautiful Buffalo," as Leo Pusateri refers to our mutual hometown. When I met Leo there and learned about his Value Ladder™ and related concepts, I saw immediately that they could help my fellow CPAs answer these questions and offer them a workable strategy for better understanding themselves and their clients.

When people choose a CPA firm, they look for technical expertise and quality client service, but you and I both know that there's more involved. Your clients pick and stick with your firm because of the important connection they have made with you. It is a special bond, one that can even span generations, but one we rarely think much about. What does it encompass? Can it be transferred? Can it be taught? Can it be learned? Is it formed during the first meeting with a client or is it the result of a long history together, hashing out problems and planning for the future?

Those are critical questions for every firm because winning new clients and holding on to the ones we have is not as easy as it used to be. The consumers of our services are more sophisticated and far more educated about the many choices open to them in the marketplace. As Leo will explain in this book, that's why winging it—flying blind into the marketing arena and hoping your clients and potential clients will just *get* how great you are—doesn't cut it anymore. We're also seeing the emergence of more small firms, all of which are seeking new clients. Once upon a time, hanging out a shingle was enough to attract them, but practice development is now a much more complicated task. For new and existing firms, the key goal will be to differentiate themselves from the rest of the pack and make meaningful connections with clients. To do that, we must be able to articulate why we are uniquely qualified to help our clients address their problems and achieve their goals.

It's no longer possible for firm owners to rest on their laurels and wait for new clients to knock on the door. As the most recent Private Companies Practice Section (PCPS) CPA Firm Top Issues survey found, partner accountability has become a critical issue for many practices. CPA firm owners are expected to bring in new business and expand the services they provide to existing clients. And the old spray-and-pray technique in which you trot out all your services and hope something catches the client's attention will no longer work. Clients want to know specifically how you can address their particular needs and what benefit you will bring to the relationship.

To further reinforce the point, consider the fact that we are part of a graying profession fast approaching an uncertain retirement. Approximately 71 percent of AICPA members are over age 40, and roughly one-third of our members are age 55 or older. That means we are about to see a significant transfer of CPA firm ownership from one generation to the next in the coming decade or so. How well that transfer works depends, once again, on the connection between practitioners and their clients. In a CPA firm, ownership transfers are traditionally structured with payments made to retiring owners over 5–7 years. The retiring CPA's entire payout depends on his or her successor's ability to retain the firm's clients during that time. However, retaining a client is not a given and usually turns out to be a challenge. That's not too surprising because CPA firm owners commonly complain that their managers and up-and-coming leaders don't have what it takes to replace them. The problem is not that they lack technical skills or ambition but that these younger professionals have no experience establishing a meaningful relationship with clients based on mutual trust and respect. If that remains the case, how will this new generation hold on to the business that will cover retiring owners' retirement payouts?

As you can see, a compelling case exists for taking the time to consider the relationship that you and the other members of your firm have with clients. We live in complicated times, but the solution to at least one of our problems is simple. If we can forge and maintain that crucial bond with clients, we have a good chance of keeping them for the long term. But, as Leo says, an effective meeting of the minds depends on a meeting of the hearts. We must understand our clients' needs and our own value well enough to see how the two can work together.

That's why I'm very pleased that the PCPS has chosen to publish this book, which adapts Leo's ideas to the issues confronting CPAs. It comes at a time of great economic uncertainty, but its message is timeless: you are the value that binds clients to your firm. And the strategies in this book will help you articulate and enhance that value.

Preface

I met with a CPA buddy of mine as I was doing some research for this book. I was startled when he said, "I believe CPAs are the greatest salespeople out there." That surprised me. I was certain that if I talked about selling in this book, CPAs would never read it because they don't consider themselves salespeople. A CPA's business is about advice, counsel, consulting, providing strategic perspective, and lending a sympathetic ear. CPAs are in a trusted position, and people believe they deliver the truth and nothing but the truth.

I've kiddingly told my own trusted advisor, my CPA, that he sometimes gives me information (the truth) without a shot of novocaine. Some meetings have felt like root canals. But I needed to have someone look me in the eye, give me the straight answers, and explain my tax position properly. I needed to hear the consequences, both positive and negative, and the appropriate recommendation on what to do next. I didn't need to be sold anything, but an Alka-Seltzer, soft pillow, and massage might be appreciated on some occasions.

To top it off, my CPA delivers this news with empathy and a smile on his face. The news can be positive, or it could cause me to make some tough but appropriate decisions to protect myself, my family, and my business. Whatever the circumstance, I feel better leaving, even without an IV or medication. I know my best interests are always the top priority. The importance of that approach—putting the client first—should never be taken for granted. With one horror story after another in the financial services world in recent years, a CPA's objectivity and integrity are invaluable assets.

But that's why my friend the CPA believes CPAs are great salespeople, regardless of whether they know it. CPAs get to raise the important questions and provide the knowledge necessary to find the answers. CPAs acknowledge, clarify, and confirm. The value of CPAs' "bedside manner" also should not be overlooked. CPAs absolutely care. They truly exhibit skilled selling behaviors in a profession that is pretty uncomfortable with that word.

Selling isn't what the profession is about, but CPAs do need to be able to set themselves apart and take advantage of new business opportunities. They need to understand their own value. My CPA buddy insisted that the accounting profession needs help in competing on value. "We need to distinguish our firms better," he said. "We need to differentiate our solutions. Our business is becoming more commoditized and price sensitive as a result. Help us!

"We need to know how to sell our value. That's right, Leo," he told me, "I said SELL our value! We need other people in the community to talk us up in ways they never did before."

Call it what you want—selling, consulting, advising, counseling, strategizing—I don't care. CPAs need to think and act differently. They need to know how to keep clients, grow clients, and constantly bring in new clients. "You know what, Leo?" my friend said. "Not only do we need to know how to sell, but we also need to know how to win."

What do we mean by winning? Well, that's what this book is all about—winning. Winning when it comes to what I will refer to as "value moments of truth." Those precious moments when you have an opportunity to look a prospect or client in the eye and answer important questions that help him or her determine whether he or she will do business with you or your firm. You see my friends, YOU are the value! You make or break opportunities. The single most compelling story you need to present is the story of you, your firm, and the value you provide to clients. That story delivered at a world-class level will help you win.

If winning means hanging on to top clients and attracting new ones, then CPAs are in a great position to do it. Both of those goals require a little salesmanship, however, and CPAs think of themselves as professionals first. How, then, can CPAs sell themselves while retaining their professionalism? By knowing their own value and being able to communicate it in every business situation. That's a journey this book will help you make.

Introduction

I put the final touches on my first book, *mirror mirror on the wall am i the most valued of them all?—The Ultimate Element of Differentiation is YOU*, shortly after September 11, 2001. As I noted then, our lives would never be exactly the same. Here I sit nine years later, writing in the wake of arguably the worst financial crisis since the Great Depression. And it feels once more as if things won't be the same again. But I believe that just as the country, the business world, and the CPA profession survived September 11, we will all once again emerge from this crisis.

Crises force us to reconsider our lives and the things that are most important to us. On the business side of your life, I think it's critical to be aware at all times of what you bring to the table as a professional and how to tell other people what you have to offer in a consultative, respectful way. That's what this book will help you do.

I'm sure that the CPAs reading this must feel like financial psychologists at times. I know you offer clients a sympathetic ear before you segue into discussions about the tax, accounting, and other great services you offer. But even though you remain your clients' most trusted business advisor, your firm has probably been affected in some ways by a tough economy. Have you lost any of your valued clients? Has the communication with them changed? Is your firm under any economic duress? Are you? Or are you thriving because you take advantage of the opportunities present even in a recession to grow your revenues with existing clients? Are new clients calling even though you do little marketing just because your reputational value is so high?

As you begin this introspection, I'm curious about how you would want others in your community to describe you. What would you want them to say about you or your firm? Not just about how well you perform your services, although that's very important, but also about what you have to offer. In your consultative discussions with your clients, when you've picked up an opportunity to provide more value, has anyone ever said, "I didn't know you or your firm did that! Why didn't you ever mention that to me?" Let's hope they don't choose someone else without even talking to you. It happens, but you can avoid it.

I've told many people that my most trusted advisor is my CPA. Why? He is warm, caring, and engaged. He is extremely competent. He knows his stuff inside and out, and if he doesn't, he knows who to call to get what I need. He provides great value by going beyond the business of accounting and applying his professional eyes and ears to my personal and professional issues. He knows my family and personal situation as well as he knows my business. My CPA displays sincere interest in achieving what's most important to me, which is why I trust him. Yes, trust is the big word in our world today, and it probably always will be. My dictionary defines it best: the total confidence one has in another's integrity, character, and abilities. I trust him. In the midst of stories about the Madoff and Stanford investor fraud cases, it is a comforting feeling.

Your clients are exposing all their financial secrets to you. As a CPA friend of mine said, "We see everything." Does that make you the clients' most trusted business advisor? If not, it may be because they do not appreciate the value that you bring to the table. They may never think too much about what you mean to their success or why you are so valuable to them. This book can help you change that.

Let's talk a little about value, which is probably the most overused word in business. Yet, as overused as it is, few people who talk about it really get the importance of the concept. Few services providers really assess the value they provide. Even fewer bother to ask their coveted, most prized clients what value they perceive from their services. I'm still on my personal journey to find out how value can be talked about constantly and yet rarely taken seriously.

I know that, as a CPA, you are challenged to continue to build your own book of business. I know that in addition to the traditional tax, audit, and accounting work you provide, you may be looking to deliver value beyond the usual compliance engagements. So, what value added services are you offering? What should you be providing? Have you hesitated to add services in some areas because you're not sure how to begin?

Please fasten your seatbelts because we're going to address all these issues and more. Let's start the journey to look at this ubiquitous word— my favorite business word—value. I want to help you through unique introspection to really—I mean really—understand the services you provide and the value associated with them. If you don't know your value as a CPA, you'll never be able to properly communicate, promote, or price your value. That's true of every CPA, whether you are a member of a large firm or a sole practitioner working out of your home. Ultimately, you want to be able to control your value by building a professional practice that exceeds your clients' expectations, gives you the personal recognition and rewards you deserve, and allows you to live a life fulfilled by the value you provide to your most esteemed clients. Let's begin the journey.

No More Winging It

1

At this point, you're probably thinking, Come on Leo, how do we begin? Give me some idea of how to define my value and distinguish myself and my firm and help me win based on the value we provide.

Time out!

Let's first take care of some key concerns. We'll begin with a dreaded disease called winging it. I know CPAs pride themselves on thorough preparation and review when they offer services. You provide quality work to your clients and that comes from being on top of your game.

However, that's because you're on familiar ground when you're doing the work you've been trained to do. Once you turn to marketing or promoting your firm, or perhaps moving from traditional services to value added engagements, we're in danger of seeing more winging it.

At a recent meeting with the managing partner of a 70 person CPA firm, he told me about the difficulty of defending his business's value against competing firms when his firm is higher priced. He flat out said, "We do not know how to manage this communication. We wing it." Also, as I looked at the branding message in their office, it was evident that they were not at the black belt level when it came to articulating key points that differentiated them from the competition. Again, winging it.

Let's say it together: "No more winging it!" To discover your value and tell others about it, take a look in your mirror and begin the introspection. Ask yourself these questions to determine if you are winging it:

- Have I or my firm ever lost a piece of big business?
- Have I ever done an autopsy to find out why?
- In talking to a client or potential referral source, have I ever failed to deliver confident responses to typical questions regarding my value or the value that my firm would provide?
- Have I ever felt that I (or my team members) lacked passion in my (our) response to questions about my firm?

- Have I heard answers from other team members and been disappointed because they lacked depth or confidence or revealed a shaky understanding of the client's business?
- Have I ever felt myself hesitating to answer questions from potential clients? (I'd bet your prospects can feel your uncertainty more than you think.)

Losing business isn't quite as bad if you can look in the mirror and know you did your best. It still hurts, but not as much. That's life, and we move on. But it's different when your identical twin in the mirror honestly appraises the situation and says, "You blew it! You weren't prepared! You were just winging it."

Ouch! Now that really hurts.

Winging it occurs when you're just not on top of your game. Think about it: if the most important thing you have to sell is yourself and the value you provide, why haven't you perfected your message?

Whom Do You Admire?

Can you think of other professionals who have wowed you with their greatness? They may be role models in the sports world like Derek Jeter or Michael Jordan. You may think of Bill Gates and Warren Buffet in the business world or Tom Hanks, Meryl Streep, or Oprah Winfrey from the entertainment realm.

And as far as world-class organizations are concerned, you can't get any better than Nordstrom and Ritz-Carlton.

These people and companies work hard to distinguish themselves. They are focused and precise, don't cut corners, create memorable experiences for you, and don't wing it. As a result, you spread the word about these people and companies to others.

Think of people, companies, or teams you admire and begin your process of introspection. You can learn a great deal about how you want to conduct your own business by studying their strategies. This is a process of discovery and one that forces you to be reflective. It also challenges you to assess where you are now, where you'd like to go, and how to develop strategies to get you there.

If I called some of your clients and potential clients, would their praise for you be as passionate as your praise when you talk about some of your sports, business, or entertainment icons? Are your clients that passionate about you? Are you so dedicated to your work and the client experience you've created that they are your fervent advocates? Can they feel the love for what you do, and do they want to be a part of it? Do you clearly stand out in the crowd?

Based on our research, we've found that most CPAs haven't spent enough time in introspection to really understand their value. Is that true of you?

If you answered "Yes," do you know why you're winging it instead of delivering a consistent message to every potential client you meet? Could it be happening because you don't know your value or how to articulate it? Maybe it's because you don't take the time to develop a consistent message or prepare to answer critical questions from each prospect. Simply put, is it easier to just wing it?

If you've ever lost a big piece of business and don't know why, you need to stop taking the easy way out and start your process of introspection. You must critically challenge yourself to assess exactly where you are professionally. For example, reflect on the progress of your career and how much you're earning. Take an honest appraisal of your client base and the growth of your skill sets. Measure your career by your ability to articulate your value today. You are the final judge. Only you can give yourself the honest answers you truly require for this introspective process.

For instance, if you're already a black belt, then which degree are you? Or, if you're already all-pro, then which team are you: first, second, or third? Can you get better? Where will you be tomorrow? Where can you improve your positioning, your team, and your company? Are there holes left to fill?

The Key Behaviors

To eliminate the ailment called winging it, we also want you to concentrate on some important behaviors in your efforts to compete on value. These behaviors are confidence, passion, and speed, and they are described subsequently:

- *Confidence* is the complete understanding of the critical elements that distinguish you and the value you provide. It embodies your business approach and philosophy. You can't expect your prospects to make a confident and informed business decision if you aren't confident in your presentation. I always ask participants at my programs, what does confidence look and feel like to you? They give me a range of responses: someone who is prepared, someone who makes eye contact, someone who exudes professional competence, and someone with great experience and insight developed from years of successful client work. How would your clients rate your confidence on a scale of 1–10, with 10 being extraordinary? How would you rate yourself? Can your confidence be improved? One of the greatest takeaways from this book will be enhanced confidence.

- *Passion* is the fire you feel within yourself. It's your level of conviction. You know you're expressing yourself passionately when you speak from your heart. You're sharing what you believe, and people can feel that. They can sense that glow that comes from within you. You've heard the adage, "For he to enkindle another, he himself must glow." When is the last time someone said to you that he or she could see how much you really enjoy your work or love what you do? When people say these things to you, you know you're hitting a nerve and you've touched something inside that draws them to you.

    You don't need to stand on your chair or do something crazy to get your point across. Your clients will see your inner glow and feel it as you talk to them. Do your clients perceive that passion now? Do you love your work? Does it show, or is it just another day at the office doing what you need to do to provide for yourself or your family? On a scale of 1–10, where would you plot the power of your passion?

- *Speed* is your lack of hesitation in response. This means you don't have that awful feeling in the pit of your stomach when you're asked to differentiate yourself. If I ask you a question regarding your value, can you answer me without beating around the bush and giving me a different answer every time I ask? Speed comes from what I refer to as the "smile in your stomach." It's that great feeling of being ready for action and welcoming tough, challenging questions from people. Why? Because you've practiced and rehearsed and are ready to respond at an Olympian level of competency. I always tell our clients that every word counts. Be prepared to defend anything you say. It is that preparation for anticipated questions and the ability to deliver world class responses that takes your level of differentiation to another point on the scale of 1–10. Please rate your speed.

In addition to those three key behaviors, you also will need to learn how to articulate your answers by connecting emotionally with your clients and establishing a meeting of the hearts. This will lead to an effective meeting of the minds. This is a key tenet of all of my work. As far as the tangible benefits—those you can see, touch, and feel—here are some: you literally will increase your revenues and talk to prospects with a different sense of who you are and what you're all about. Your clients will establish lifelong relationships with you.

Taking you through our process, which we affectionately call the Value Ladder™ process, is my real value to you. I will challenge and guide you throughout the book. Along the way, gigantic light bulbs should appear over your head. I want to hear you jump and shout loud AHAs throughout your reading.

Financial professionals I've worked with say the following:

- "You helped me to connect with clients in ways I never thought I could."
- "I was able to distinguish myself in such a way that I brought in more business than ever before."
- "My confidence has increased. I'm talking to people at levels I've never reached before."
- "I'm controlling client meetings differently. I'm getting deeper emotionally with them."
- "I'm at peace with myself after 20 years of thinking I was in the wrong business."

Well, those are the rewards that keep me going every day. Now, that's real value.

Let's start working on your confidence,
passion, and speed.

Discovering the Value Ladder™ 2

I've discussed a few key concepts so far: winging it, confidence, passion, and speed. However, what I believe sets me apart is my dogged dedication to helping people in the profession of consulting and, yes, selling take their ability to compete on value to levels that they have never experienced before. As a CPA who needs to know his or her value and the price of that value, you are not only an indispensable consultant for your clients but also someone with the potential to be—excuse me, folks—a great salesperson. That means being able to sell your value.

We have seen a renewed focus on value in recent years—a value revolution, in fact. Many authors are writing about the value revolution and their interpretation of it. I have read their books, and they occupy an honored place on my bookshelves. I also was influenced by some friends and fellow consultants with their iterations of the word *value*. I have spent years of my life earning the equivalent of a doctorate in the challenges we all face in trying to stand out and to differentiate our firms, our solutions, and ourselves. I have performed my own internal introspection to learn how to become my best; raise my confidence level; and, in the process, help others excel and enhance their confidence. The real value of this journey, as I say, has been amazing. Seeing organizations and individuals competing on their value, winning client mandates, and feeling better about themselves has been my finest reward for many years.

The moment of illumination for me came when I was teaching a sales training class that focused on helping clients ultimately become confident with their salesperson. My intellectual and life AHA hit me like a ton of bricks. "That's it," I said to myself, "we all want clients to have confidence in their decision to work with us, but, how can they if, in fact, you, the one consulting or selling to them, are not confident?" We need to be confident ourselves before we can expect someone to feel confidence in us. Bingo. That confidence would bring with it passion and, ultimately, speed in answering questions. The end result? No more winging it! My business career and reputational value went to a new level as I worked relentlessly to share this insight with my clients.

That, my friend, is how a stunningly simple, remarkably elegant, but deceptively difficult model was created. It became known as the Value Ladder™, seven questions that professional services providers are being asked by today's more sophisticated and informed clients who have a broader range of service options at their disposal.

An old adage says the best way to learn how to sell is first to understand what it's like to buy. Think of the logical questions you might ask before making an important buying decision for your business or for yourself and your family. Common sense tells you that you want to know more about the individual or the company you are considering. You want to know what they do. For example

- is their background impressive, both professionally and personally?
- do they specialize in what you are looking for?
- why are they doing this?
- what drives their thinking?
- what have they learned from successfully working with other clients?
- is their story compelling?
- can you feel their passion?
- if you decide to work with them, what is their process?
- who else have they done this for?
- who are their typical or ideal clients?
- can you call somebody for a testimonial?
- what success have they had?

When you're making an important purchase, don't you feel more comfortable when you understand the answers to these questions? As your conversation deepens, especially if you're shopping around, you may want to find out what makes the seller different. "I want to know more about your company," you may say. "I want to hear about your products, services, and solutions. How do they distinguish you from your competitors? And, oh, by the way, I may want to know more about you as an individual. What do you stand for? What can I expect from working with you? And why should I make this decision to do business with you? What is the real value?"

If you are like me, you want to make a confident decision about someone who is confident in themselves and their business. Throw in some passion and spontaneity in responding to all these queries and you've got the makings of the Value Ladder™.

Spelling It Out

What, exactly, is the Value Ladder™, anyway? The Value Ladder™ is a process consisting of seven strategic steps (critical questions prospects usually ask or might be thinking) that prompt you to be introspective, ultimately helping you enhance or develop your compelling story of value. It is the core component of a strategic development initiative that helps you begin a discovery process that will enable you to differentiate your value from the competition. It helps you deliver your message with confidence, passion, and speed (lack of hesitation). The behavior change? No more winging it. The outcome? Winning. Winning by keeping and growing valued clients and bringing new valued clients to your firm. That's real value!

It sounds straightforward and logical, and it is. That's the power of the model: it's simple and liberating. You can reply to most prospects' questions with one of the seven answers. Developing your seven answers will arm you for any situation.

When I actually started creating the Value Ladder™, I decided to go off-site for a strategic workshop with key members of my team to brainstorm and role-play. Where do I even begin, I thought? How do I get people to elevate their game? How can I help organizations and individuals learn how to truly compete on their value? How can I raise their levels of confidence, passion, and speed? How do we eradicate the dreaded disease of winging it? How can I help people win?

The First Step on the Ladder

I needed a starting point, so I thought, What is the most basic question people ask when they first meet someone new? It's "Hi, what's your name?" or "Tell me a little bit about yourself." How many times can you remember meeting someone and after all of the who are you-type questions, the next one usually was, "What do you do?" Most people say, for example, "I'm a CPA" or "I'm with XYZ accounting firm."

I always tell people who answer this way, "No, I know who you are, but what do you actually do?" Sometimes, they confuse who they are with what they do because in today's society, you are what you do.

If you can concisely answer the question, "Who are you?" in a way that is compelling and differentiating, it will make an immediate impression on your prospect and go a long way toward forging the first strong emotional connection. It's also important to remember that the way you respond to the question is critical.

So, just who are you? Well, we'll get into the nuts-and-bolts of who you are and how to articulate this a little later in the book. It's your mission to give your prospect a tight definition of your organization, business, or practice background with as much passion as you can muster. Your response must set the stage for the prospect to go to the next question on the Value Ladder™, which is, "What do you do?"

The Next Logical Steps

As I continued to role-play with my team during the workshop, I realized that the second step on the Value Ladder™ ("What do you do?") became the early prompt to stating the Unique Value Proposition™ (UVP™). The UVP™ is the single most important statement capturing the essence of what you do in a way that sets you apart from your competition.

As I moved through the process of developing the Value Ladder™, it dawned on me that as we dissected and expanded the first two questions, we were unconsciously jumping to the eventual fourth question, which was on how do you do what you do. I realized that something was wrong because a step was definitely missing. I noticed that in my role-playing, I would automatically answer the following question—the next logical step—"Why do you do what you do?"

This question is very important because people want a quick story of why, even though they may not pose the question in quite that way. What they want to know, in essence, are your core business beliefs. They want to learn what makes you or your organization tick. They want to know what motivates you and what compels you to be in this business. This is where your story comes alive. Thus, the next logical point on the Value Ladder™ became the why portion, which we immediately included in the seven critical questions.

Next, we developed the question "How do you do what you do?" This is the fourth step. A prospect might ask, for example, how you would work with him or her or his or her company. A prospect may also ask you to explain your process. This is where you position and illustrate your process to demonstrate that you are a black belt financial professional. I'll illustrate in detail a little later how this step on the Value Ladder™ works so beautifully.

So, as you continue climbing up the Value Ladder™ (as we did in our own development process), you begin to understand how the questions and your answers become a finely tuned process. If you are talking to a prospect and you get to this point on the Value Ladder™, the prospect usually will ask the next question, which is "Who have you done it for?" Or, more to the point, "Who else do you work with? Am I a typical client? Am I the type of person you could help?" He or she will want to know about the successes you've had and if you have worked with people similar to him or her.

Next, your prospect will want to know "What makes you different?" This is the sixth step on the Value Ladder™. You need to be able to distinguish yourself on three levels: your organization, your solutions, and yourself. Here's where the theme of differentiation starts to come alive. As I explain fully in an upcoming chapter, your prospects may be interviewing a number of competitive alternatives, and you will need to know how to properly distinguish yourself from them. Ultimately, your response to this question will help prospects and clients understand the depth and breadth of your differentiation and establish you as being world-class.

The seventh and last question is "Why should I do business with you?" Here, a prospect is asking, "What's your real value to me, and what am I going to get out of this partnership?" My belief, as mentioned earlier, is that business becomes a meeting of the hearts first and then a meeting of the minds. Real value may be measured qualitatively or quantitatively. The qualitative measurement is emotional; it's the heart-to-heart connection. The quantitative part is logical; it's the intellectual connection. Understanding how to connect emotionally and logically is critical. If you meet both the emotional and intellectual needs of your clients, you are providing real value. This question helps you differentiate yourself on both levels.

A Complete Message

The seven questions began as a commonsense way of articulating my own introduction, message, and call to action to prospective clients. I'm proud to pass them on to you. You'll see that they work beautifully!

The Value Ladder™ simply helps the normal flow of conversation. Once you have the answers to all seven questions down pat, you'll be able to further refine your critical responses on defining your value and differentiating yourself from the competition. When you answer all seven questions, you develop a complete message that sums up your value. It is not some simple elevator speech; prospects get a sense of the totality of who you are and what you represent.

But I must tell you that discovering and delivering your value is a strategic process. It's what I refer to as a chess game of questioning, answering, and understanding. You have to be able to move the pieces around, connect the dots, and make sure your answers are integrated and seamless from one step to the next. As an introspective discovery process, the Value Ladder™ process allows you to understand the seven critical questions clients ask and answer them with confidence, passion, and speed.

You will learn how to be flexible, in the moment, in control, and quick on your feet during your client meetings. You also will learn how to meet the needs of your clients while answering those seven critical questions. Plus, you can immediately implement these skills as you learn them.

The Value Ladder™ also can be viewed as your virtual file cabinet. What do I mean by that? Read on to understand the simplicity of this model and its similarities to the many files and filing drawer cabinets in your office. The biggest difference is that this virtual file cabinet will eventually become the most important one in your office.

The Virtual File Cabinet™ — Custom Answers in a Drawer

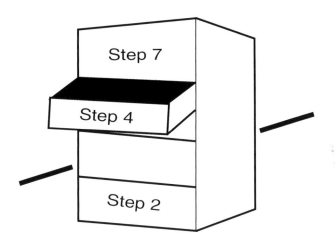

Think of the Value Ladder™ as your very own custom seven drawer virtual file cabinet. To better understand this concept, visualize the file cabinets you have in your office. They are probably organized into client files, competitor files, marketing files, financial information files, and so on. Most likely, they contain identical manila folders, separating your important information. I'll help you build your virtual file cabinet as we go through the book, but first, here's a preview of how it works.

Simply stated, each drawer in your virtual file cabinet equals one question on the Value Ladder™. Visualize the seven drawers labeled with the names of the seven questions. In each drawer are your virtual manila folders containing the many ways you can answer each question. For example, if your first drawer is labeled "Who Are You?" then you will have folders in that drawer labeled "Business Background" and "Personal Background," both with as little or as much information as you may need at the appropriate moments in a client presentation, and so on for the remaining six questions.

As you continue to climb the Value Ladder™, you'll have to think about your answers to each question as though you were building or creating your own virtual file cabinet. (I'll provide examples for you in each chapter.) You need to take this file cabinet with you everywhere—from prospect meetings to client meetings, from charitable events to social gatherings, from golf outings to elevators, from trains to plane trips. You never know when a question might pop up. Trust me, questions will come up everywhere in one way, shape, or form.

In chapter 11, you'll also find six powerful applications for the virtual file cabinet to help you further deliver your message with confidence, passion, and speed, and chapter 12 will introduce you to creating a culture of value in your firm. Chapter 13 describes the key questions that will engage and challenge senior leaders before they create an organizational Value Ladder™, and chapter 14 helps you set some priorities.

Now, it's time to start climbing the Value Ladder™!

The   Value   Ladder™

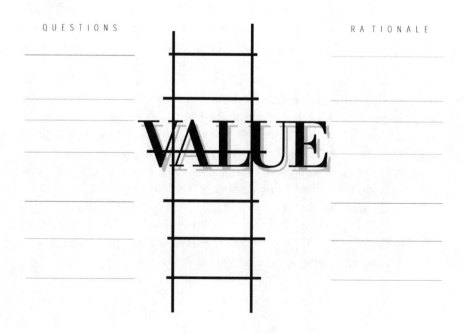

QUESTIONS   RATIONALE

The   Value   Ladder™

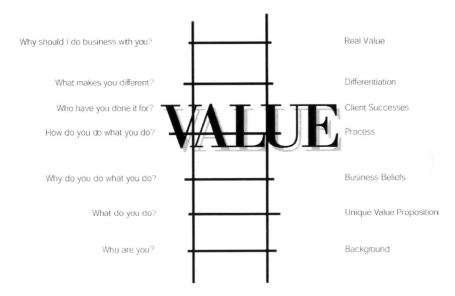

Why should I do business with you?	Real Value
What makes you different?	Differentiation
Who have you done it for?	Client Successes
How do you do what you do?	Process
Why do you do what you do?	Business Beliefs
What do you do?	Unique Value Proposition
Who are you?	Background

Who Are You?

3

Imagine meeting someone for the first time. The setting could be an informal social get-together or a formal business opportunity. As the saying goes, you only have one chance to make a great first impression. If that's the case, then why wouldn't we want to do our best to get off to a good start? Why would we, in some cases, wing it?

It has amazed me over the years to see people struggle with this. Or they may challenge the importance of making this first emotional and logical connection. It's not about me, Leo, they say, it's about them, meaning a prospect or client. Who cares about me, the cynics say. I want to know more about them. No need to waste time on me when I have an opportunity to learn about others. They don't need to know anything about me, especially personal stuff. Let the games begin, they say.

I disagree. Slow down and think about this for a moment.

It is an act of professional respect to properly introduce yourself and your organization to others. People are making a big decision when it comes to choosing a CPA or CPA firm to manage their tax, audit, accounting, consulting, personal financial planning, or other requirements. As this step of the Value Ladder™ will demonstrate, you need to use your own intuition about how much information you should share. But trust me, be prepared. Like a great actor who wows his or her audience or any professional seeking new business, you must script your openings to ensure you get off to the best possible start. Do yourself a favor and take charge of something you can control.

Who are you? Those are three words that sound simple and ask a simple question. But is it really? This is the first critical question that begins your journey up the Value Ladder™. You'll need to stay on this bottom rung for a while, though, until your answers are so engaging that your prospect will genuinely want to know more about you. If your prospect doesn't ask, that means you haven't properly set the stage and that you'll quickly lose his or her attention.

When someone asks about your background, how do you respond? Often, that person really wants to know what you do and not just your name and title, as the question implies. More often than not, this simple question is asked in many different ways.

For example, how many times has someone said to you, "Tell me a little bit about yourself," or, "Tell me more about your background." He or she may want to know how long you've been a CPA or been in the accounting profession and may want to know more about your business experiences. On a personal level, he or she may want to know how long you have lived in your current area. If a person isn't asking these types of questions, he or she is probably wondering about them.

It's important to have responses for the many ways people may use to learn more about you. This is when you can truly pull out the appropriate response from your file drawer in your virtual file cabinet.

As you read through this chapter, you'll learn how to establish immediate credibility with your prospect and how to articulate your organization's, business's, or practice's background and, if and when appropriate, your personal background. I repeat: if and when appropriate.

First, let's do some thinking about who we really are and the types of things that make a lasting impression.

First and Lasting Impressions

When you answer the question, "Who are you?" and identify yourself in a confident and passionate way, giving the other person a genuine sense of yourself, you make a powerful emotional connection that creates a lasting impression. That's why it's so important to have a consistent response to all of these questions because it sets the stage for your continuing discussion with the prospect.

"Who are you?" is, quite literally, the first question out of the gate, and you don't want to wing it right off the bat. Some might call it dancing around the subject, which is a kissing cousin to winging it. Others might say beating around the bush. No matter what you call it, it's all just hesitation and an obvious lack of confidence in yourself and your message.

Think about how powerful it is to look a prospect in the eye when they say, "Tell me about yourself" and you deliver a precise answer.

What are the five top things you would tell a prospect to introduce your-self and your organization? Do you immediately know what you would say without any hesitation?

What would you say if David Letterman or Ellen DeGeneres put a microphone in your face on TV and asked, "Who are you? Tell me a little bit about yourself." Could you answer without hesitation? Could you answer with confidence, passion, and speed? Could you be precise without gulping and searching for words and without dancing or wing-ing it?

Respond to the Situation

The answers you give when questioned should prompt further questions from prospects. Remember, you always should be in the moment and flexible with your responses. Here's an example of what I typically say when I'm asked about who I am.

"I'm Leo Pusateri, the president of Pusateri Consulting. We are a boutique sales consulting and training organization headquartered in beautiful Buffalo, New York, and we specialize in, and partner with, financial service organizations and financial entrepreneurs to help them compete more effectively on the philosophies of value." The key words I've underlined have special meaning and are ones I consistently use in my message. My clients might laugh when I talk about beautiful Buffalo, but they remember it and me. The same goes for the words *boutique, specialize, partner,* and *philosophies of value.* I want people to ask me about these words. Called drill downs in our programs, these words prompt follow-up questions. When you are totally prepared, this really gives you an opportunity to share or show your confidence, passion, and speed.

A person might ask how long I have been doing this or might ask about my background. So you see, even though they begin by asking who I am, they often will pose further questions and go deeper, wanting to know more about me both personally and professionally.

I always tell CPAs that it's not necessary to share all of the informa-tion at once. Use your common sense and intuition and only share details about yourself if it is appropriate. The key word here is *appropriate.*

Your intuition will always tell you how much is enough. You don't need to be a motormouth. You don't need to say, "Let me tell you everything about my business and personal background." This might not be the appropriate situation to talk about things such as civic activities, family, education, and special interests. It all depends on the emotional connection you're making at the time. In each client situation, you have to intuitively assess how much is appropriate. Experience will make it easier to do this over time.

Think about how you would respond to the, "Who are you?" question. Does your response position you as the professional you want your client to perceive you to be? Does it help create further dialogue and trust? Does it build rapport with your client?

As you prepare to explain who you are, it's very important to remember that the way in which you respond makes that critical first impression.

How Do You Rate?

At one of my presentations, there were many successful people in the audience. I decided to try an experiment. I asked the audience, "On a confidence continuum, on a scale of 1–10, how would you rate yourself? Number 1 on the scale would be 'No Confidence.' The fifth level might be 'I'm somewhat confident, but I need help.' The highest level, number 10, would be 'I'm Michael Jordan, Wayne Gretzky, get out of my face because I can answer this question with the best of them. I have confidence.' Where do you feel you are on this confidence meter?"

1	2	3	4	5	6	7	8	9	10

As I went around the room, the participants (remember, many were very successful entrepreneurs) were rating themselves at 8, 9, and 10. Every now and then, someone would rate themselves as a 3 or 4, so I was prompted to ask, "You folks are very successful already. I'm curious, why would you rate yourself so low? Are you just being tough on yourself or what?"

Several confided, "As successful as we are, we know it still is something that we take for granted. We wing it." You need to get out of the gate with a powerful start. If you don't, your prospect may quickly tune you out way before the other six questions can be answered.

Getting Off to a Strong Start

The Value Ladder™ concept takes off immediately with everyone with whom you come in contact. When you talk to them, they are instantly forming impressions of you. As you climb the Value Ladder™ and continue to trust the process, you'll return to the early questions (such as, "Who are you?") with even better perspective. I have seen individuals reach the sixth step on the Value Ladder™ ("What makes you different?") and suddenly realize there are common themes running through all the answers to the Value Ladder™ questions.

If you called 10 of your clients and asked them to describe you, would their responses reflect the same themes as your answers to the Value Ladder™ questions? If you feel confident, self-assured, and knowledgeable, would your clients say the same things about you?

Find a quiet place where you can think about, and write down, the answers to the question, "Who are you?" Here are some guidelines to follow:

- Give your name and title, then for whom you work.
- Describe your organization. Provide the firm's history, clients, strategic alliances, relationships, and how long it has been in business.
- If you're part of a team or a department, identify it.
- Describe your team's or department's function and explain how it operates and your role in it.

If you feel it is appropriate—and please let me repeat here, only if is appropriate—you may want to present the following information to your client, as well.

Professional Considerations

- Your location
- Years with current organization

- Members of your team
- Former employers
- Key clients
- Areas of expertise
- Professional designations or special education
- Professional affiliations
- Special background
- Recent annual business growth or other firm successes
- Other considerations

Personal Considerations

- Where you live
- Where you grew up
- Family information
- Educational background
- Hobbies
- Sports you enjoy
- Other nonwork activities
- Charities or civic organizations

I have found that many people take these considerations for granted and don't realize how much they say about them. Those who personally reflect on the question, "Who are you?" will find the stage set for the introspection that continues toward developing your Unique Value Proposition™.

To practice what I preach, the following represents the summary of my own personal introspection on the first Value Ladder™ question— "Who are you?"

- Leo Pusateri
- President
- Pusateri Consulting
- Boutique Sales Consulting/Training
- Headquarters: Beautiful Buffalo
- Specialize . . . Partner . . . Philosophies of Value

Professional Considerations
- Unique Background
- Xerox Learning Systems
- Elias Asset Management
- Narrow/Deep Approach to Business
- Competing on Value

Personal Considerations
- Married 31 Years
- 4 Children
- St. Bonaventure University
- Community Commitment
- Golf
- Coaching people to be their best

Jot down some ideas on what you should be emphasizing when introducing yourself.

Get Visual

Are you a visual learner or an auditory learner? Most people who I work with are visual learners. They learn best by seeing things, not just listening. So I wondered how I could have some fun here. I then took my background answer and illustrated it with pictures.

I use this selectively in presentations, but I can assure you that people smile, laugh, and nod their heads positively as I tell my story. My company and my professional and personal background come alive through pictures. It will humanize you and, I promise, it will distinguish you. Get creative as you think about this approach. Do me a favor and think out of the box and have some fun.

Empowering organizations and individuals to discover, articulate and capitalize on their unique value.

Xerox Learning Systems
+
Elias Asset Management
=

Competing On Value

KNOW / PRICE / SELL / LIVE

Pusateri Consulting and Training

From left: Jeff Liebel, Susan Burton, Nicole Wickings, Leo Pusateri, Giles Kavanagh and Sue Peace

Pusateri Canada

Brent Wagner

If you were putting together a slide show that summed you up for your clients, both professionally and personally, what would it look like? Maybe it would include a picture of your town, as I have, or the office building of which you're proud. Maybe one slide would show the logos of some of your top clients. You'd want a picture of your family, possibly involved in some favorite activity. Putting together the slide show will help you clarify and remember some of the key points you'll make when you tell clients who you are. It also can serve as a fun backdrop to presentations for prospective clients or you can post it on your Web site or in your office.

On the Spot

Now that you've thoroughly examined who you are with thought-provoking questions, it's a good idea to test yourself on how well you could present yourself in a real situation. Remember, you don't want to practice on your prospect, so practice now.

Strategic Questions to Consider

- How well do I position myself now? Is it easy for the people I meet to understand my value as a professional?
- What is my typical response to the question, "Who are you?"
- How does my response help to begin my differentiation process?
- How does it set the stage for further dialogue, building trust and rapport?
- If I'm in charge of a team or organization, what other information do my team members need if I want them to give an impressive answer to this question?
- If my team and I can answer this question at a world-class level, what impact will this have on our dealings with clients, prospects, and other business contacts?
- What impression will I make in the marketplace if members of my organization fail to respond to this question with confidence, passion, and speed?

This is a good time to remind you that your virtual file cabinet comes into play here in very important ways. Remember, your first drawer is titled "Who Are You?" and you should have a manila folder labeled

"Business Background." You should have another one titled "Personal Background," and both files will include information you can repeat frontward and backward to convey your message.

The beauty of the virtual file cabinet is that you can visualize the key points you want to make and virtually pull from your resources the material you need to make your presentation more powerful and compelling.

A Case in Point

I was asked to conduct a Value Ladder™ workshop for executives of two leading-edge firms attempting to finalize a strategic partnership. However, they couldn't agree on how their combined marketing professionals should position this new endeavor. We addressed our Value Ladder™ questions with similar frustrations because it was difficult for them to agree on a cohesive message. It didn't surprise me to hear that the proposed partnership was never finalized.

The introspection beginning with, "Who are you?" is strategic discovery at its best. Don't take this question for granted. It's like blocking and tackling in football—basic but critical. Adherence to discipline and mastery will set you apart. If you can't settle on a response to, "Who are you?" then you might as well forget about trying to answer the remaining questions.

Tell a Compelling Story

Look in your mirror. Spend some time reflecting. "Who are you?" is an easy question to answer on the surface, but with proper introspection and reflection, you soon realize how deep your self-analysis can go. You'll be surprised at what you'll learn about yourself by going through this exercise. You'll uncover aspects of yourself that you previously didn't think of revealing to even your existing clients.

Discovery starts with that first step and, in turn, will give you ammunition to make a powerful first impression. It's much like reading a good book. To keep you turning the pages, a book must capture your interest or curiosity immediately, but it also will hold your attention all the way to a dynamic and satisfying end.

One of the most important lessons you can take with you after reading this chapter is this: a compelling response to the question, "Who are you?" will automatically lead your prospect to ask, "What do you do?"—the next question on the Value Ladder™. If your answer to this first question is thought provoking enough to leave the prospect wanting to learn more, then you have perfected the answer to the first step on the Value Ladder™. Each Value Ladder™ question, in essence, acts as a springboard for the next one.

No matter how good you think your answers are, more opportunities exist to make them even tighter. Just as you have a virtual file cabinet, you also can grab a virtual screwdriver to make needed adjustments to your story. If you want to go from good to great to extraordinary, it will require ongoing alignment of all your answers to ensure the perfect response. Keep an open mind, and hold on to your screwdriver as you go through all the questions on the Value Ladder™.

Final Thoughts

Use unique language (your own lexicon) that reflects you and is memorable.

I bet you still remember beautiful Buffalo. What do you want people to remember about you?

You only have one chance to make a great first impression.

Don't wing it!

Don't get ahead of yourself.

Seize the opportunity to differentiate yourself right off the bat. This step begins the process of setting you apart.

Look for a theme in your professional and personal background.

What makes it special? A passion for being my best and coaching others to be their best is mine. What is yours?

Every word counts.

Imagine the audience for your message and polish it accordingly so that it captures their attention.

Think ahead.

If you say something, be prepared for any appropriate follow-up question. This is where you really start to stand out. It's not what you say in the elevator that is most important; it's the conversation that ensues that really makes the difference.

Enumerate where possible.

I have these responsibilities. I'd like to point out these three things regarding my professional background. Be prepared to give specifics that back up what you say. Your prospect will admire your confidence and articulation.

A good background answer should focus on just the facts.

It begins to position your value and also builds credibility for you and your firm.

Now you should be prepared for the second step ("What do you do?") and the development and creation of your Unique Value Proposition™ (UVP™).

Let's get to work on your UVP™!

What Do You Do?

4

So here we are at the second question on the Value Ladder™, which is "What do you do?" I've described this question as one of the fundamental questions of life. You meet someone and, invariably at some point in the conversation, one person looks at the other and curiously asks, "So, what do you do?"

"Well, I'm a CPA," you might say. Or you might say, "I'm an accountant, and I work for one of the accounting firms in town (or in the area, city, community, and so on)." You answered the question, and you know that people are familiar with the work of CPAs. However, did you really distinguish yourself? Did you really explain or describe what you or your firm members do as CPAs? Did you give any sense of the value that you provide to your clients? Probably not, if you are like most CPAs.

Did you ever stop to consider how many CPAs there are in the United States? In fact, there are more than 350,000 members of the AICPA, and roughly half of them are in public practice. In the United States alone, all the CPAs would fill the Rose Bowl in Pasadena, the new Cowboys Stadium, the Louisiana Superdome in New Orleans, and Rich Stadium in the beautiful Buffalo area. (Forgive me for my hometown bias because I am a long term masochistic Buffalo Bills season ticket holder!) So, what's the point, you say?

We've all agreed in earlier chapters that people perceive the business as more commoditized. You need to stand out. Many firms are offering value added services based on the specialized talents of some partners or other team members. After a few boom years, some of you may be finding that you only grow by taking business from each other. You golf at some of the same country clubs. You laugh over a $2 Nassau when you are matched up over a weekend round and fight each other during the week for coveted local clients. And, yes, you are finding that someone had the nerve to lowball the pricing of his or her services to win an important client. Although the accounting profession is discussed using words that describe people of good character (*trust, professionalism, integrity,* and so on), CPAs also are subject to words that other industries accepted years ago (*competitive, cutthroat, hyper-price sensitive,* and so on). Need I say more?

With that competitive environment in mind, again I ask, what do you do? What do you really do? And yes, please tell me what value you provide to your valued clients.

So, all of you CPAs who passed through the turnstiles at the stadiums I mentioned, would you look to your left and right and say, "We all do the same thing. We look the same (wear the same jerseys or suits) and talk the same." Is that how you think of your profession? I doubt it.

So, if you're a little different from the next CPA, what value do you offer me, I ask. Or, finally, what's your value proposition, and, strategically, is it unique? You see, every CPA or accounting firm should have a value proposition, and it should be unique. The second step of the Value Ladder™ is all about developing your Unique Value Proposition™ (UVP™).

Defining Your UVP™

What exactly is a UVP™? It is a brief statement or paragraph that clearly and concisely captures the essence of what differentiates you from your competition. It is your compelling message delivered with such confidence, passion, and speed that you stand out in a crowd.

You know the great feeling you get when someone looks you in the eye, is unbelievably conversationally proficient, speaks with respect, is precise with his or her words, and customizes and personalizes the dialogue at a high level? Well, doesn't that make an incredible impression on you? Don't you feel like you're dealing with someone who is the consummate professional? Someone who is a peak performer and has invested time, energy, and money getting down the unique branding of his or her practice or team. You can feel the all-star aura of that person, right? You leave with the feeling that the person connected with you and that he or she asked the right questions and had his or her act together. Wouldn't you like your prospects and clients to feel this way about you? Of course you would!

As we outline the step-by-step process of creating your own UVP™, it will become clearer to you just how important and critical it is to capture your prospect's attention. Your UVP™ is a powerful statement. The exercise in introspection to discover and develop it is important, but you also will be learning how to articulate it with confidence, passion, and speed. Our experience has taught us that mastery in articulation is a strong differentiating factor. People can feel it when you believe in what you are saying.

It's not easy to create a confident, succinct statement. This is the most frustrating and challenging part of the seven steps to conquer; however, once completed, it is a true high-five experience. Let's break down the individual words (*unique*, *value*, and *proposition*) to get a clearer picture:

- *Unique.* You are one of a kind, or as I say, you have exclusivity.
- *Value.* How well your solutions help achieve your client's goals.
- *Proposition.* Your written or verbal proposal.

In essence, your UVP™ is your statement of what you feel you do so uniquely well in providing your value to others. How can we be unique when there are 350,000 others with the same credential? Just as each person has his or her own fingerprint and DNA, CPAs and firms do, as well. Sometimes, the words firms use to describe themselves are eerily similar. You can easily tell, though, which firms live the words. I believe it's actually easier than you think.

Your UVP™ sets the stage for your differentiation, and it should tell your prospects that what you do is special. It should generate interest and give a definite sense of your expertise. It also should open the door for people to ask more about what you do or what you mean by a UVP™.

A UVP™ is not a tagline, slogan, logo, or corporate mission statement. It should, however, say what makes you special and tell your prospects and clients about your world-class business. A branding phrase such as Nike's "Just Do It" is a great advertising slogan, but it is not a UVP™. Your UVP™ is longer than a tagline but not as comprehensive as a mission statement—it's the best of both. Other close relatives to the UVP™ are positioning statements, vision statements, and selling propositions. I always tell participants in our programs not to get caught up in the semantics. Ten different consultants may call it 10 different things.

Just get your best answer down without excuses. The story you have to tell about yourself and your firm should be a great story well told.

In previous chapters, you've learned that discovering your value is an introspective process. It takes deep thought and consideration, and it involves many drafts, not just simply jotting down notes on a sheet of paper. As you continue through this chapter, I'll give you examples of UVPs™ and step-by-step guidelines to help you create your own.

What would be a UVP™ for a CPA or a firm? For those with a particular specialty, it might be the following:

- "We partner with medical professionals to enhance their practices and their own personal finances."
- "I offer auto dealerships the business planning and management they need to grow their companies."
- "We help not-for-profit organizations maximize their resources so they are better able to achieve their missions."

To reach out to individuals, you might say the following:

- "We provide clients with the expertise and insights to address tax and personal financial planning concerns and meet their long term financial goals."
- "I help people make sense of the financial aspects of their lives."

There might be as many UVPs™ as there are unique CPAs and firms, so let's not get ahead of ourselves in putting one together just yet.

There can be two types of UVPs™: one for an individual and one for a firm. If your organization already has its own UVP™, you should determine if it's appropriate to use as is or if it needs refining. Usually, a single UVP™ for a CPA firm is all that's needed; everyone should be "singing from the same sheet." We'll talk more about firm and individual UVPs™ later in this chapter.

What Do You Actually Do?

When you really think about your business strategies, the types of people you want to work with, and the kind of professional and personal life you're trying to create for yourself, you find it's that much easier to see what you truly do. That's what happened to me when I realized in my own career that the more I increased my focus, the more I knew why I was unique and how to position myself in this world.

Once you identify what makes you unique, it's fairly simple to create your UVP™ and answer all of the critical questions asked by your clients. My UVP™ says it simply: "Empowering organizations and individuals to discover, articulate and capitalize on their unique value."

Here's the real key: it's so much easier to answer the question, "What do you do?" when you speak from your heart and soul. You'll find you exude more confidence about your special gifts and talents.

Making It Come Alive

You must create a UVP™ statement that you can use in both business and personal situations. This does not mean you should repeat the exact same language word-for-word each time. Once you have the basic foundation for answering the question, "What do you do?" you can customize your statement to the situation or person. That's when you should go into your virtual file cabinet, pull out the appropriate response, and make it come alive with your confidence, passion, and speed.

For example, if you met someone on the golf course and he or she asked what you do, you probably wouldn't recite your exact written UVP™. You want to be conversational, friendly, and make the words meaningful to the person you are addressing at that moment. The better you have your answer down, the easier it will be for you to personalize your UVP™ for each conversation. However, most of what you deliver will be taken from your basic message, which should be consistent time after time.

Let's say that your UVP™ is one of the ones we mentioned: "We provide clients with the expertise and insights to address tax and personal financial planning concerns and meet their long term financial goals." So, you might tell your new golf buddy, "I'm a CPA who works with people like you to address tax and financial planning concerns. My firm has particular expertise and advanced credentials in this area, and we work with clients to identify their financial goals and help them achieve them."

That's how the conversation would work with an individual client, but let's look at what you might say if you met a business owner on the golf course and this was your UVP™: "We offer clients reliable, accurate financial information that they can use to make timely decisions and pursue their strategic goals." In this instance, you could say, "I'm a CPA. Of course, you know that we help our clients with things like financial statements and tax reporting. But we also work with them to maximize their financing options, analyze acquisitions, expand into new markets, and meet a host of other goals."

Remember that this conversation might take place over the course of an entire afternoon, so you might not be robotically reciting these or similar words. The main idea is that your UVP™ will embody certain key points that you will express in conversation, as appropriate in the moment.

A good way to decide how you want to frame your answer in any given situation is to consider this question: after you've delivered your answer to this person on the golf course, how would you want him or her to describe you to someone else? Think about this for a moment. What type of message can you deliver in 10 seconds? Did you create an aura that would lead this person to tell his or her spouse, friend, or colleague that you were really impressive? In our preceding examples, the CPAs on the golf course were confident in, and knowledgeable about, their firms' abilities, showed enthusiasm—or passion—about them, and didn't hesitate in their responses. Their new friends will come away with a great impression.

Here's another example. Imagine you are on a plane making polite conversation and the person next to you asks, "What do you do?"

I might respond by saying, "I'm Leo Pusateri; it's nice to meet you. I'm from the beautiful Buffalo area, and I own my own boutique sales consulting and training firm that specializes in the financial marketplace. I work with a lot of prestigious companies and individuals who are challenged to distinguish themselves. They want to earn and win business from people like you."

Based on my intuition about the person's interest I might add, "This is a crowded marketplace today. I help clients answer questions about what makes them different and why people should do business with them. I've developed a company that helps individuals and firms answer those questions at levels they have truly never thought about before."

That whole statement takes approximately 15 seconds to deliver, and I made my UVP™ come alive. Read it out loud and you'll see what I mean.

Imagine instead that I told that same person, "Hi, my name is Leo Pusateri, and I do sales training." Do you think he or she would have the same understanding of what I really do? What does sales training actually mean, after all? It could mean anything. That's an example of the fact that we often don't know how to answer the question at the highest level of conversational proficiency. In the CPA profession, you might sometimes say you're a tax accountant or an auditor. These responses seem to answer the question, but they don't really express what you do for an individual or business.

To be sure, sometimes the situation calls for the "short and dirty" version. That said, you must be careful not to answer who you are (someone who does sales training) instead of what you do (someone who works with prestigious companies and individuals who are challenged to distinguish themselves.)

Go on Through

One unforgettable UVP™ moment occurred at the Peace Bridge in the beautiful Buffalo area. Returning from a business trip in Toronto, my business partner, Giles Kavanagh, and I were leaving Canada, tired after a successful day and each anxious to get home for some downtime. Not so easy though with a by-the-rules, sunglasses-wearing, equally tired Customs and Border Protection officer. Try to picture this scene: Giles driving and Leo in the passenger seat getting impatient.

Citizenship? *U.S., sir.*

Where have you been? *Toronto.*

Purpose of your trip? *Sales meeting with a potential client.*

Bringing anything back? Anything to declare? *No sir, nothing. (Leo starting to get agitated.)*

Do you have cash or monetary instruments over $10,000? *No, sir. (But wish I did.)*

Who do you work for? *Pusateri Consulting, a sales consulting and training company based here in the Buffalo area. (Please let us through. I'm exhausted and I've got to go to the bathroom.)*

So, what do you guys do? *Finally, the eureka moment. My Managing Director Giles effortlessly said, "We empower organizations to discover, articulate, and capitalize on their unique value."*

Customs and Border Protection officer finally loosens up, smiles, and eventually says the magic words "Go on through."

The moral of the story is never be ambiguous with Customs and Border Protection officers. At the same time, as CPAs, never be ambiguous with your prospects. Someone may finally loosen up to you. Their version of "Go on through" may be "Let's talk further; we'd like to find out more about you, and we might want to do business with you."

You should always look for opportunities to customize or personalize your answer based on to whom you are talking. Other variables that will affect your answer include where you are in the conversation and the opportunity to say something in that unique situation that really connects with the people with whom you are in discussion. Let's return to the first example we discussed earlier of the CPA on the golf course who does financial planning. Based on the circumstances, here's what he might add to his UVP™: "I heard you joking earlier about saving for college because you have kids entering middle school. I sure know what you're facing there. College planning is one of the services we provide for clients. We get great satisfaction out of setting up plans that reduce our clients' worries about how to pay for their kids' education."

The second example we discussed earlier involved a meeting on the golf course with a business owner. Here's how the CPA might extend the UVP™ for the potential client: "You mention that you are preparing for an audit and not looking forward to it. In our audits, we have a year-end services delivery planning process that's second to none. We minimize the stress for our clients and deliver a customized year-end services work plan. We finish not only with the audit report but also with an analysis of the client's business that he or she can put to use immediately." You're getting across your core message, but you're tailoring it for this particular business owner.

However you state it, be sure to protect the integrity of your UVP™. For instance, in my case, I've answered the question about what I do with statements like, "We help people like you to answer that very same question for yourself, with increased confidence, passion, and speed." Or, "We help senior leaders like yourself truly learn how to distinguish your firm by unifying your culture around your compelling story and, ultimately, helping you win more client mandates." In every case, it conveys the same message about my firm.

Five Steps to Your UVP™

Let's get started developing your UVP™. The first step is to think about the various words that describe the unique value of your firm. What does your practice do that makes it unique or gives it a possible competitive advantage? Here is a sample listing of words that might come up when you think about what you bring to the table:

- Specialist in tax, business planning, audit, or any number of services or industries
- Trusted business advisor
- Offer clients a competitive edge
- Cutting-edge expertise
- Respected credentials
- Objectivity
- Competence
- Integrity
- Global perspective
- Regional or local knowledge and outlook
- Strong knowledge of, and credibility with, local bankers or other funding sources
- Large but entrepreneurial
- Small but offering full service
- Active in the community and socially responsible
- Long history in the community

If I gave you 60 seconds to brainstorm some ideas, what would be the key words on your list? Give it a try. Remember, this is brainstorming. Come up with as many ideas as you can. Strive for quantity, not quality. Don't second-guess yourself, defer judgment, and have some fun.

The second step is to consider the words that best describe the unique value of the solutions you provide your clients. Here are examples of words that convey what you do for them:

- Personalized service and attention
- Responsive to client needs
- Peerless customer service
- Easy access to firm professionals
- Innovative solutions
- Comprehensive
- Customized
- Reliable, accurate results

There may be some overlap from these questions, so don't get too concerned. Remember, you are only brainstorming. Again, if I gave you another 60 seconds to come up with ideas, what would be the key words on your list? Keep going. You've got some momentum now.

Third, think about all the words that describe the unique value of you as an individual, your team, or your firm. What can clients expect from working with you? What do you stand for? Speaking from the client's perspective, what can I expect if I entrust my tax and wealth planning strategies to you? How will choosing you as my auditor help me improve my business? What can I expect if you handle my business planning? Here are some words that might apply:

- Skillful	- Informed	- Trustworthy
- Proficient	- Trusted	- Aware
- Experienced	- Expert	- Distinctive
- Capable	- Master	- Understanding
- Intelligent	- Competent	- Smart
- Clever	- Prepared	- Accomplished
- Resourceful	- Sharp	- Efficient
- Compassionate	- Methodical	- Talented
- Discreet	- Ethical	- Sophisticated
- Innovative	- Educated	- Honest

Take another 60 seconds to brainstorm some additional words to describe the value that you or your team provide. Is there anything else you would add to this list? Not only are you possibly coming up with answers for the second question here, you are gathering words that will be useful for all steps of the Value Ladder™.

Now that you have a list of key words, your fourth step is to choose up to 10 that really jump out at you. Use them as a starting point for the first draft of your UVP™.

The fifth step is to begin writing your initial draft. When you are satisfied with the first version, review it carefully and make any changes you feel necessary. Have a colleague read it. Leave it for a few days and then go back to it with a fresh outlook. A final UVP™ comes together as you continue to climb the Value Ladder™.

Why not ask for input from your most valuable resources—your current clients? To do so, just pick up the phone. Better yet, visit them. Nothing is better than a face-to-face meeting to catch up on details, as well as convey a thank you for their business. It's also a nice time to get feedback from them regarding ways you can improve.

Other questions you might ask are as follows: Why did you hire me? What were some of the key points that led you to work with me? How would you describe what I do for you? What do you value the most in working with me? What is the real value I provide to you? I'm not completely kidding when I challenge my clients by saying, "Ask these questions and shut up!" Just listen, acknowledge, clarify, and confirm. You might just be surprised by what you hear.

It's critical to keep a sense of what's important to your clients so you can continue to provide the value that's vital to them. You need to be sensitive to your core marketplace. Plus, it helps you refine your UVP™ as your clients change and the marketplace evolves.

Here are a few guidelines as you begin writing your draft:

- Make your UVP™ 1 sentence or a brief statement. As a general rule, it should be between 10 and 20 words.
- Be specific.
- Convey a positive, passionate, and confident feeling.
- Use your words to promote an emotional connection.
- Make a statement that creates enough interest and excitement so that someone will say, "Tell me more about that."
- Put your UVP™ on the back of your business card. Here's mine, as an example:

pusater!
discover your value

Leo Pusarteri
President

6255 Sheridan Drive, Suite 100
Williamsville, NY 14221 USA
+1.716.631.9860
+1.716.631.9471 Fax
pusatericonsulting.com
leo@pusatericonsulting.com

*Empowering organizations
and individuals to discover,
articulate and capitalize on
their unique value.*

Be prepared to answer your prospect's follow-up questions. You want to emphasize certain words in your sentences to make your message memorable, so be ready to expand on them upon request. This will really help make your UVP™ come alive.

It's also important to edit and rewrite because as you do, your UVP™ becomes more concise and clear. Continue reviewing your draft until you get it right.

It's not necessary to have more than one UVP™, even if you serve different markets. You are who you are and you do what you do, regardless of your markets. The manila folders in your virtual file cabinet will help you customize your answers to questions germane to specific market segments when the occasions arise.

To help spark your creativity, let's think again about some more sample UVPs™ that might be used by CPAs:

- I provide business information that helps clients reduce taxes, lower unnecessary costs, seize opportunities, and make critical decisions.
- We offer customized business strategies based on a thorough knowledge and understanding of our clients' industries and help them reach their financial goals.
- We provide audits (or reviews or compilations) that spotlight new opportunities and challenges to be addressed.
- I offer comprehensive, objective financial advice to clients who desire a high level of personal service.
- We enable individuals to make more informed decisions about their money, the growth and protection of their assets, and their estate and other planning needs.

Are you starting to get a feel for this yet? What would you say to an important prospect?

The UVP™: Yours, Mine, and Ours

Should everyone in the firm have their own UVP™? Ideally, there should be one UVP™ for the entire firm that articulates the value that the firm brings to clients. Once you have a firm UVP™ in place, however, you should challenge each firm member to consider his or her own role in making the UVP™ come alive for his or her own clients.

Think about a firm whose UVP™ is one of the ones we mentioned earlier: "We offer customized business strategies based on a thorough knowledge and understanding of our clients' industries and help them reach their financial goals."

A CPA who works in the firm's health care practice might adapt this UVP™ to say the following: "We use our thorough knowledge and understanding of health care organizations to help them maximize profits and opportunities and reach their financial goals."

What if your firm does not have a UVP™ and you are not a firm leader who can put one in place? No problem. You can still create your own UVP™ that can be the foundation of your individual dealings with clients.

Referrals and Existing Clients

Imagine you have an appointment with a referral. Are you prepared to deliver a consistent answer to the question, "What do you do?" Is the answer similar to the one you gave the person on the plane or golf course? Most likely not. You might be thinking, "Well, I really don't need to explain a lot about what I do because this prospect is a referral who already knows what I do." But I ask you, Are you sure he or she really understands what distinguishes you from the competition?

Remember, too, that UVPs™ can not only impress prospects but they also can open up new opportunities with existing clients. Many clients may not understand the breadth of your services. Here is an example that illustrates the point.

A CPA, Linda, had done accounting and tax work for a large manufacturing client, Sheila, for many years. Sheila recommended Linda to a buddy of hers, Ken, who owned several retail shops. Sheila accompanied Linda when she met with Ken. As Linda told Ken about her UVP™ and the full range of her services, Sheila's eyes widened in amazement. "I thought you just put together forms I had to have, like tax returns and financial statements. But your UVP™ says you can help me grow my business and lower my costs. Why didn't you tell me you could do that?"

As a result of the conversation, Linda was able to expand her services to Sheila and bring on Ken as a new client. Because Sheila became a client long before Linda developed her UVP™, she might never have known about the firm's many services if it hadn't been for the referral. Although many clients may be able to tell others that you create a spiffy tax return, they may not be in the best position to talk about your unique value to potential referrals. Don't make assumptions about what a new referral—or even the client who recommended you—understands about your value.

Staying on Task

Let's say you are now in a business meeting. You most likely talked through the initial pleasantries. You've built rapport and maybe you've both talked about your respective backgrounds. At the appropriate moment, you should then say, "Now, I'd like to spend a few minutes to walk you through my UVP™ (or your firm's UVP™) or to properly explain to you the value that we provide to our most valued clients."

At this point, you would say something like, "We partner with businesses like yours (or families like yours). We establish and deliver a comprehensive tax planning (or business consulting) process that will put us on the same side of the table, working together as partners. This will promote the successful attainment of many of your long term goals. That's what we do."

You can see the effectiveness of your UVP™ from this dialogue. You can never spend too much time on discovering the answer to the question, "What do you do?" Learning how to articulate that answer with complete flexibility and being in the moment will give you much more inner confidence because you know who you really are. When you understand your UVP™, it's a lot easier to say no to certain prospects (when necessary). When you are on task and on purpose, you are delivering your UVP™ to the marketplace you covet.

Stay on task for the type of business and lifestyle you are trying to build. The process is based on the best possible introspection, evaluating the full uniqueness and importance of the total package you are selling—you.

Strategic Questions to Consider

- Do you have a UVP™?
- If yes
  - are you and your firm or team able to articulate your UVP™ with confidence, passion, and speed?
  - is it a clear and consistent statement, targeted for your market?
  - how was it developed?
  - who was responsible for developing it?
  - what process did you use to develop it?
  - when was it developed, and is it still appropriate?
- What is your typical response to the question, "What do you do?"
- Is this the best response? Does it serve your purpose?
- What, specifically, do you want to gain from your response? Is your firm's or team's response targeted to achieve your specific goals (for example, distinguish your firm, gain new business, and so on)?
- Where is the UVP™ used?
- If you have no UVP™, do you or your organization have the following other kissing cousins of the UVP™:
  - Tag line, label, or slogan
  - Brand strategy
  - Selling proposition (or unique selling proposition)
  - Mission or vision statement
  - Values statement

Final Thoughts

Don't just say what you do. Tell people what makes you unique.

Your UVP™ should sum up the benefit that you offer to clients in a way that captures their attention.

The UVP™ is not like other messages.

Longer than a tagline or slogan and shorter than a mission statement, it is concise but powerful.

The UVP™ is a stepping stone for conversation.

Instead of reciting the UVP™, learn how to adapt it to each new situation.

To support this compelling story even further, let's explore your business beliefs.

Now, let's climb the next step on the Value Ladder™.

Why Do You Do What You Do? 5

So, now we know who you are. You have made a great first impression by avoiding a simplistic, canned answer about your background and offering real depth. We also know what you do or what your accounting firm does. You've articulated your Unique Value Proposition™ (UVP™), and oh, by the way, you looked me in the eye and were able to extend the discussion of your value with confidence, passion, and speed.

Now, as we climb to the third step on the Value Ladder™, I need you to think about a question that begins with the word *why*. "Why do you do what you do?" The answer to that question can be found by thinking about your business beliefs. What are they? They're the things that experience and years in the business have taught you. They're also the wisdom you have learned from your research and work with clients on similar issues plus your best bets about future trends in your business and your clients' companies. These beliefs are connective themes that tell a prospect what you or your firm are passionate about. They represent your strongest convictions. They are emotional, and when expressed properly, they will help you win business.

Imagine a client or prospect walking into your office or conference room. Prominently hung on the wall are your business beliefs. His or her eyes are laser focused on the words in this picture because he or she knows that they matter. They tell a story and really depict what drives your thinking.

Well, what do you believe so strongly that other people will get goose bumps when watching you perform or listening to your story? In other words, why do you do what you do?

Why?

It's arguably the most thought-provoking word in the English language. It forces us to think deeply and answer with heartfelt conviction. Why we do what we do is very personal to us, and it can be a tricky step to teach on the Value Ladder™. Sometimes, people jump the gun and will answer, "Because I love my job, that's why." Or they might say, "Because I love helping people, and I care for my clients."

On the surface, those responses sound good. However, a better answer would contain the convictions that support the professional services you present to your clients, not how you treat your clients. That's a big difference. Why you do what you do should be reflected in your business beliefs. These beliefs are your philosophies behind key offerings to clients, whether traditional or consulting services.

I tell CPAs in my program that of course I care about my clients. I treat people with respect, and I have integrity. But that's not why I do what I do; that's what I stand for. Those are some of my standards and core values. Just because you are passionate or accountable, that doesn't tell me why you do what you do. It just tells me what I can expect from working with you.

Subtle but important differences exist in how this question can be answered. We'll discuss the distinctions in detail a little later. As you eventually distinguish these differences in your model, the answers become very powerful when delivered.

But the question for you is, "What do you believe?"

What's the Foundation for Your Business Beliefs?

Your business beliefs can be expressed in different ways. Whenever you're asked your opinion, in fact, you may end up stating your beliefs.

Think about sources for this answer from outside of your worklife. Sometimes it's easier to start there and come back to what you do every day in your profession. If you are married, what do you believe are some of the successful traits of a solid, happy, loving marriage? If you are a parent, what are the keys to developing great relationships with your kids? If you are involved in a worthy cause or support a local charity, what gets you so excited and passionate about it? If you admire a team of any kind, what makes that team so successful? Consider the totality of your experiences. Perhaps you see traits in the people on a school board of which you are a member or maybe you've had a positive experience working with a world-class company.

When you think about your answer to this question on the Value Ladder™, remember to focus on why you recommend certain strategies or approaches. Keep in mind that your business beliefs should relate to and support your UVP™. A tight connection between your UVP™ and business beliefs will take your differentiation to a higher level. Business beliefs are based on four factors.

First, you need to take into account the direction in which your organization or practice is headed, which may be affected not only by circumstances in your business but also by the regulatory, business, and investment climate and trends in the profession and industries you serve. This exercise can help you get a clear picture of how to structure your business beliefs to support your UVP™. Here are some questions to consider:

- Are you positioned to respond to changing circumstances?
- Are you attempting to differentiate your firm in a crowded marketplace?
- Are you maximizing the potential in your current client base?
- Are there other service opportunities open to you?
- Are you ready to compete on value?
- Are you consulting with clients or are you still simply helping them meet their compliance needs?
- Are you perceived as a run-of-the-mill service provider or the client's one-and-only trusted advisor?
- How do people know and talk about you now?

Second, business beliefs also are founded on where your business has been, which means looking at the following historical patterns:

- Do you earn your fees and revenues on an hourly rate?
- Do you regularly compete on price or value?
- Do you focus on traditional services?
- Have you positioned yourself to offer other value added solutions and develop a proactive marketing strategy?

Third, what have you learned as an organization? What opinions, wisdom, and experience have you developed in your firm? What have your clients taught you? To answer these questions, consider the following:

- What you know works best for your firm.
- What you have learned works best for your clients.
- What working with clients has taught you over the years.

Here's another question that will help you consider your business beliefs: what are the biggest mistakes you have seen your clients make over the years? For example

- making short sighted business or money management decisions.
- failing to make business decisions at all and simply allowing their companies or personal finances to drift forward.
- taking on too much debt.
- failing to minimize their tax burden.
- allowing opportunities to pass them by.

Fourth, sadly, business beliefs can be formulated in another way. As we all know, unexpected events in your life or business can change your outlook, as well as your answers, within seconds, minutes, and hours. The loss of a loved one, the departure of someone you've mentored who decides to leave your firm, or a health scare are a few examples of these events. They make you reevaluate your life and business and also could shape the urgency and force of your convictions. How have life changing experiences shaped your business beliefs?

The Question Unfolds

Because a prospect or client will not always ask you a Value Ladder™ question verbatim or outright, be prepared for this question to be stated in a number of different ways, such as the following:

- What has led you to do what you are doing today?
- Why do you feel this is the best way to help someone achieve his or her goals?
- Tell me why you feel so strongly about what you do.
- Give me a compelling reason why you are in this business.
- What have you learned from this business?

Here's how you might reply to the last question: "Having been in the profession for 15 years, I've seen good economies and bad ones. I've seen businesses grow and thrive and some that have truly struggled. I've learned a lot over the years from working with valued clients like you. I believe you really need a serious focus on the long term right now. Your business strategies (or financial planning choices, if you're talking to an individual) do not support your goals."

What you will find is that you are now "telling a story." It's much like a feature film that's moving along. Your goal is to provoke your prospect into expressing interest and asking for more information.

Getting at the Core Beliefs

I do what I do because I truly believe certain truths. I have five core business beliefs. They form the compelling story of my business; totally support my UVP™; and, as you will see in the next chapter, link perfectly to my process.

Be specific when you define your business beliefs. For instance, be precise in numbering and ordering them. You should know whether you have four, five, six, or however many. Don't take this for granted. Here are mine to serve as examples:

1. *There is a value revolution going on.* It is alive and well and being led by the most important people in your business life—your clients.

2. *I believe the changing client is driving the value revolution.* They have many characteristics, most notably an awareness of their many competitive options.

3. *I believe your business is becoming more commoditized, and the challenge to distinguish yourself is critical.* Clients are faced with a dilemma today due to all the competitive options. Other CPA firms are lining up to take their business, and other organizations are eager to handle their tax or financial planning work or audit or accounting needs. To the changing client, everybody looks the same and talks the same. It is paramount that you make an outstanding effort to distinguish yourself.

4.   *I believe that any organization or team or individual in business today needs to answer seven simple yet powerful questions to truly distinguish themselves based on their value.* We call these questions the Value Ladder™ because we believe answering them all embodies the full essence of your organizational or team or individual value.

5.   *I believe we must stop winging it in offering responses to clients and answer questions with confidence, passion, and speed.* To truly distinguish yourself, you should develop world-class answers to questions about the most important thing you have to sell—you. These answers need to be delivered with the highest levels of confidence, passion, and speed (remember, it's not a matter of how quickly you speak but lack of hesitation in response).

These are my core business beliefs. You'll notice I didn't say anything about my own passion, commitment, trust, respect, or value. That's because those things describe how I or my team are individually different. They reflect core values that I live my life by and that my company also lives by. These core values are different from my business beliefs.

So, what are your business beliefs?

CPAs and Business Beliefs

Now that I've given you some good ideas about business beliefs, start brainstorming about the elements of your own answer to "Why do you do what you do?" Here are more examples of what other CPAs have listed as their core business beliefs:

- Smart financial decision making depends on timely and accurate information.
- We can and should be our clients' trusted business advisors.
- Financial success begins with understanding the core values and goals of my clients.
- Even the smartest managers sometimes need help understanding the next best steps for their business or in their personal financial planning.

- Objectivity is a valuable asset.
- Most clients do not operate their businesses day to day with real profit maximization in mind.
- Many business owners do not have a clear picture of how they really make money.
- Most business owners suffer too long before asking for professional help as their finances become more complex with growth.
- Most individuals take a piecemeal approach to financial planning, making it more difficult for them to achieve their short and long term goals.
- Saving clients some money on their taxes is not enough. Tax planning should lead to a broader discussion of wealth, estate, or retirement planning.
- Performing an audit or a review or compilation are not enough. We add value when we offer clients some perspective on what the numbers actually mean.
- Retirement of the baby boomers means that many of our clients need help with succession planning in their businesses and retirement and estate planning in their personal lives.
- Our profession is extraordinarily well positioned to help with the baby boomers' wealth transfer.
- Many CPAs focus too much on the numbers and not enough on what produces them.
- You can't change the past, but you can shape the future.
- Clear-eyed planning can connect people to their dreams.

This is not meant to be a comprehensive list, but it is meant to help inspire you to develop your own list of beliefs.

I challenge my clients to create a business belief booklet. This booklet contains your or your firm's core business beliefs plus possible belief categories. A summary page of the business belief booklet might look like this:

Core Business Beliefs

I (We) Believe:

Biggest mistakes our **clients have made** 1 2 3 4 5	1	**Risk Management** **Perspectives** 1 2 3 4 5
	2	
TAX STRATEGY PERSPECTIVES 1 2 3 4 5	3	WEALTH MANAGEMENT THOUGHTS 1 2 3 4 5
THE KEYS TO SEIZING OPPORTUNITIES 1 2 3 4 5	4	BUSINESS SUCCESSION THOUGHTS 1 2 3 4 5
	5	
PERSONAL FINANCIAL GOALS ACHIEVEMENT 1 2 3 4 5		LONG TERM PLANNING 1 2 3 4 5

This is strictly an example. You can use whatever sections make sense for you and your firm.

Team Up

You may already have a list of ideas and feel ready to finalize your own set of business beliefs. Before you do, it might be smart to team up with a partner or colleague so you can both share ideas. Start by presenting your beliefs to this partner the same way you would present them to a prospect. Allow your partner to ask questions (and vice versa) about each of your beliefs. Having someone you trust act as your prospect gives you a safe environment in which to practice delivering your message.

As your partner asks questions, be prepared to go deeper into each belief concept. This is important. For each business belief or key word, ask to be challenged, and be prepared for follow-up questions. Employ the same process here as you did with your UVP™. As I've said before, you should never take lightly any question asked or opinion sought from you. They are all opportunities to really tighten up your story and consultative skill set.

Once you have identified your business beliefs, revisit your UVP™and rewrite it if necessary. As you did with your UVP™, be prepared to do some editing and critical evaluation of your business beliefs. For example, say that "Objectivity is a valuable asset" is one of your beliefs. Should objectivity be mentioned in your UVP™? If so, how would you include it? Does it work with the message you have there now? How does it fit in with your other business beliefs and UVP™? This is the time to take out your virtual screwdriver to tighten your thoughts and refine your message.

Your business beliefs must be consistent with the solutions or process you market. Prospects and clients can spot inconsistencies right away.

After Who, What, Why—Are You a Fit?

After discussing your background, stating your UVP™, and sharing your business beliefs with a prospect, you may discover something very important. You may find that you're just not compatible. Sometimes, the chemistry just isn't right. This may not be a relationship either of you want to pursue.

If so, this is okay because we all need to develop and maintain relationships with those who share our values, beliefs, and passions. You know that if you look at your own client base, you will find clients who don't really fit your firm. You may keep them on for various reasons but no need to add more.

If a prospect does share your business beliefs, then you can proceed to climb higher on the Value Ladder™. By this time, the prospect should be eager to hear all about how you do what you do, which is the next step on the Value Ladder™.

Strategic Questions to Consider

Take a few moments to reflect on what you've read in this chapter. Give a lot of thought to what you have written so far about your business beliefs. Before you finalize them, ask yourself these strategic questions to help sum up what you have learned so far:

- What are my core business beliefs?
- Have I given them priority in my business life?
- Where are my business beliefs written or posted?
- Can my team, partner, or assistant articulate these business beliefs?
- Can I take my business beliefs to the next level when a prospect asks me, "What do you mean by that" or "Tell me more"?
- Can I articulate them with confidence, passion, and speed?
- How do my beliefs affect the way I do business?
- Do they help drive my business and keep me in focus?
- Do I use my business beliefs in my marketing and sales materials?
- Do my clients know my business beliefs?
- What impact might they have on my prospect's decision to do business with me?

Remember, it's best to pinpoint exactly how many business beliefs you will ultimately call your own. Be precise. How many can you fit in your virtual file cabinet? You don't want to overload your folder drawer.

Final Thoughts

Beliefs showcase you.

You will be amazed at the reaction of clients and prospects when you nail this answer. Sharing your convictions could literally win you a client or a firm mandate.

Short beliefs can be more memorable.

Go back and review the list. I bet that as you read them, some of them stood out for you.

Beliefs should hold together to tell a story.

If Steven Spielberg, Martin Scorsese, or Ron Howard, great Hollywood film producers and directors, were filming your beliefs, would the story move them? Do your beliefs logically flow from one to the next? You should feel the power in them as you read your own. Put some music to them and maybe you have an Oscar award winner in the making.

They should pick up on your UVP™.

I always say it is critical that your answers seamlessly connect from one to the next.

Enumerate.

A definite power exists in enumeration. For instance, my firm has five business beliefs. Enumeration shows people your confidence. You are prepared with your list of convictions, and winging it never entered your mind or your client's mind.

Now that you have a better understanding of your business beliefs, the next logical question from your clients will be "How do you do what you do?" It's time to climb the Value Ladder™ to question number four to discover your answer.

Keep that screwdriver handy!

How Do You Do What You Do? 6

Who, what, why, and now how.

So, how do you do what you do? What is your process? Think about where we are now on the Value Ladder™. You've introduced yourself. People are comfortable with you, your team, or your firm. You've discussed your Unique Value Proposition™ (UVP™). Your prospect has a comfortable understanding of your core competencies. A lot of head nodding has been done and important questions have been answered. You've also opened up your heart and shared the convictions that drive you from within. People can feel what you believe and are reassured by these beliefs. They are quietly thinking that they know you, understand what you do, and have a strong feeling for what you are passionate about. Let's keep talking, they say.

"So, where do we go from here?" they wonder. "How would we work together?" Or maybe they are talking to another CPA firm and are trying to compare you and your services to a competitor. Every word, regardless of whether you know it, is being evaluated, similar to when you make an important decision.

Your process is a key step, if not the most critical one, in differentiating your value. In essence, your process is what exactly you will do that will let a client experience your UVP™.

Buying the Process

In your own mind, you can easily imagine the kinds of services you could offer any given client, how they will map out, and what they will do for the client or his or her business. But the client can't read what's in your mind. At this point in your discussions, the client likes what you're saying, but it's still unclear how it will all come together. You've shared a lot of great ideas and you've shown your confidence, passion, and speed, but at least somewhere in his or her mind, the client is still thinking, "How exactly is this all going to work?" The client may have a general idea of what it means to work with a CPA and what any given service might entail. However, the client wants to know what will happen when he or she does business with you and your firm. In a world full of qualified professionals, that's what's going to set you apart.

This is the point where you have to help the client make the leap to buy the process. I can speak personally about this step because I've done it myself. Yes, that's right, I bought process! "How can you buy a process?" you may wonder. I actually made a decision to move a significant part of my own net worth to a financial planner based on his process.

I have had numerous discussions with my CPA over many years regarding my big picture wealth planning. My CPA, as I have mentioned, has been my ultimate sounding board, my voice of reason. He has been there every step of the way as I have built my company, and he has attended to the growing needs of my family. For a long time, though, one thing has been missing: an integrated, long term wealth strategy. For many years, I felt that I didn't have a plan that coordinated the efforts of my CPA and trust and estate attorney. This is something I have neglected to set in place.

So, when my CPA challenged me on my long term plan, I was ready for someone who had a great process. My CPA has worked closely with a key financial planner friend of mine, John Moshides. (Depicted here is a copy of his unique process; used with permission from John Moshides, president of Moshides Financial Group.)

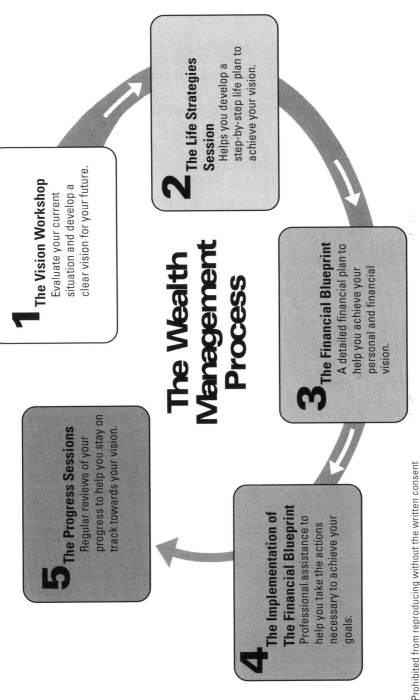

The Wealth Management Process

1 The Vision Workshop
Evaluate your current situation and develop a clear vision for your future.

2 The Life Strategies Session
Helps you develop a step-by-step life plan to achieve your vision.

3 The Financial Blueprint
A detailed financial plan to help you achieve your personal and financial vision.

4 The Implementation of The Financial Blueprint
Professional assistance to help you take the actions necessary to achieve your goals.

5 The Progress Sessions
Regular reviews of your progress to help you stay on track towards your vision.

I ultimately decided to give him a great deal of business because of his tight, professional process—one that can be explained and acted on. Think about this from a professional standpoint. Would you, as a CPA, be more comfortable recommending a professional with this type of an approach or someone who says, "Well, we, uh, uh, you know, we have typically, uh, four to five steps that we do, sometimes, uh, you know it depends on, you know, uh"? Stop it. You're killing me. I'm losing my will to live listening to a professional who is winging it.

But, unfortunately, some CPAs wing this step, as well.

Simply put, a *process* is a system of operations or of creating something or a series of actions, changes, or functions that achieve an end or result. The processes you highlight in attracting and retaining new business can help differentiate you from the competition based on how well you or your team, or both, make them come alive. The business idea that it's not what you do but how you do it especially holds true here.

Do you have a process? Are there steps you take to ensure that you understand each client's needs, marshal the right resources to meet them, and monitor their changing status so your plan continues to work? "Yes, of course," you say, "those are the kinds of things any professional CPA firm would do." Okay, then, can you explain your process to clients and prospects? If not, how do you expect to develop and grow your business? I'll help you discover and cultivate a process that will differentiate you from your competition and help you win more high level business. We'll go into detail toward the end of the chapter with some important exercises to help you do this.

A Key Element of Differentiation

You're in a meeting, you've just explained the first three steps of the Value Ladder™, and your prospect says, "Everything sounds great. What's next? Where do we go from here?" Some prospects may have already talked with two or three competing firms, and the conversation might go something like this: "I was speaking to a competitor and he said he had a methodology. His firm has a client service system that he explained to us. What's yours?" or "The CPA I spoke to last week had a very comprehensive five step process for business planning. Do you have one?"

These are the types of questions that come up when you're on the fourth rung of the Value Ladder™. If they don't come up, they are still buried somewhere in your client's mind. You will need world-class answers to all of them.

Your unique process is a key element of your differentiation. Both you and your prospects have a process: your prospects use one to make a buying decision, and you use one to develop new business relationships and retain and grow your client base. When you're making a personal buying decision (that is, a new house or car or a family vacation), you have a particular thought process to help you make those decisions.

Many successful, committed CPAs already have a process, but I've known quite a few CPAs who do not. They just wing it. I've seen many successful financial professionals at my retreats who've said, "I'm here because, after hearing your presentation, I realize I don't really have a process or a way to properly deliver it."

Your Process: What Does It Look Like?

Okay, now it's time to define your process. In my training sessions, I ask participants to brainstorm all the things they believe are part of their process. To help generate ideas I ask, "What would you say to a prospect if he or she asked, 'What is your process?'"

Start thinking about (or listing) components of your process. These may include steps such as the following:

- Organizational readiness or preparing for the engagement
- Getting to know the client by identifying financial needs and establishing goals and developing a strategy for the engagement
- As necessary, pulling together a team to perform the engagement
- Creating a written game plan
- Enacting the plan and meeting the client's needs
- Performance reporting
- Long term goals discussion to plan for future needs
- Constant monitoring and communication with the client

List as many steps as you can. Then, working alone or with your team, depending on the engagement, put them in a logical order and think about how you would explain them to your prospects.

Now try to illustrate it. Don't just describe it but think about how you would bring the steps to life. For example, can you graphically walk a prospect through your process? Start drawing. Use your imagination. A picture is worth a thousand words. Illustrating your process helps solidify its value through visuals and storytelling.

Next, take a look at the chart that follows. It depicts what I call the client relationship process. Study the four areas for identifying your process. We've printed the chart here so you can follow along.

Client Relationship Process

1: Step By Step	2: How Do We Go About Doing This?	3: Differentiation Factors	4: Adding More Value
Step 1			
Step 2			
Step 3			
Step 4			
Step 5			
Step 6			
Step 7			

Column one allows you to list up to seven steps in your process that differentiate you from your competition (most clients I coach have from four to six steps, but five is usually the magic number).

Column two asks for your explanation of each step in your process. What are the specific actions you would take to complete each step? How do you make these actions come alive for someone outside your firm?

For example, in a financial planning engagement, how do you accomplish the client's objectives? Do you use a specific planning approach developed by you or your firm or do you use third party soft-ware? Do you ask certain types of questions? In an audit, what steps do you take to ensure that the outcome is both accurate and reliable and the process is as painless as possible for the client? Give some thought to all the services you offer. List all of the things you do. Remember, the key question in the client's mind as you describe each step is what's in it for me. The client doesn't want to know the nitty-gritty details of how well your firm is managed or what kinds of research materials you use. When the client is listening to you talk about your steps, he or she wants to know how each step provides a benefit that enhances his or her financial life or makes you a better fit for his or her needs than the competition.

Column three is where you list all of the ways you or your organization are different from the competition. This step is more difficult and calls for deeper analysis. Think of your core competitors. Is there a benchmark that sets you apart? Are you familiar with their process? Are there any things you do that you believe are exclusive or give you a true competitive advantage? Does your firm do things that your competitors don't do? The more you can identify these differentiators, the better.

Column four allows you to include additional ways you or your organization can add more value within each step for your prospects and clients. Is there anything in your process that you can change to make it even better? Authors Robert J. Kreigel and Louis Patler challenge readers in their book, *If It Ain't Broke . . . Break It!: And Other Unconventional Wisdom for a Changing Business World*. Sounds like the kind of unconventional wisdom that just might work in a changing world.

Don't just say to your prospect, "Yes, I have a five step process." I say to you, let's go to process school and really get your differentiation down. Let's take each step so deep that by the end, you'll feel as though you have your doctorate in process.

You alone make this process come alive; prospects are buying you. You are the most important reason a prospect will commit to working with your firm. As the title of this book says, you are the value! You make this decision a memorable experience for them. Then, as a bonus, this prospect becomes an advocate because he or she feels so good about the relationship.

It's like being a golfer who says, "I really have to get good at the short game. I have to get better at hitting my driver, fairway woods, or irons or in my course management." The golfer has to practice to become the consummate professional, and each of those steps is part of a process that helps him or her do so. It works the same way for you. You may have five steps in your process, but the problem, as I see it, is that most CPAs just take them all for granted. Because the steps become so automatic and you're so familiar with them, some of the excitement starts to wear away.

Often, you will hear that your prospect is talking to a competitor with a similar process. So, what should you say? Most times, it may be how you say something rather than what you say. In this situation, here's what I would tell a prospect who is questioning me about a competitor. (Throughout the book, our prospect will be named Mr. P.) "Well, Mr. P., I'm glad to hear you're speaking to a CPA who espouses a process. Anyone you talk to should be able to look you in the eye and properly explain how he or she will work with you and what you should expect."

Say it with passion and in a way that makes your prospect feel good about it. That way, you reinforce that he or she is right to be doing his or her homework and that you would expect no less from him or her. But when you follow up with your own story, make it come alive with a delivery that demonstrates confidence, passion, and speed.

Begin by completing at least the first two columns of the client relationship process chart to get your hands around your process. The last two steps (three and four) may take some time to complete, but keep thinking about what makes your process different and how you can make the steps even more powerful and take them to another level.

A Case in Point

My firm is constantly working on our process. Just when you have it down pat, you learn something new from a client that may actually further tighten what you do. Our process is called the Real Value Experience™. It builds off our UVP™ and business beliefs. It seamlessly integrates from one answer to the next, and yours should, too. A graphic representation is presented subsequently with a description of the steps.

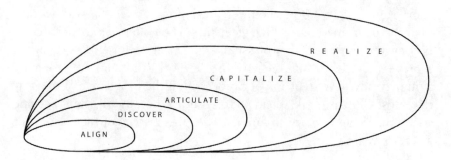

Align

Are we all in total agreement about the end game? Do we understand what is keeping you up at night? Have we looked at how value is perceived and delivered at every level of the organization, from senior leaders to clients? Is your team excited to get started? Do we agree on how we will measure success?

Discover

Are you ready to be challenged to reinvigorate your organization and reignite the flame of differentiation and value? Are you prepared to develop simple but compelling and, above all, differentiated answers to seven key questions? Do you really know your real value?

Articulate

What's the use of having a great message if not everyone in your organization can articulate it with high levels of confidence, passion, and speed? Moreover, can they do it in a way that preserves their entrepreneurial spirit? No more winging it! That's the simple mantra here.

Capitalize

Are we prepared for and willing to do what it takes to win? Can you deliver value in every client interaction? Are you getting closer and closer to completely aligning yourself with clients? Do you truly know what your clients value? Are you aligning your value to what your clients are telling you? Oh, by the way, have you priced it correctly?

Realize

It's time to fully realize your value, create a culture of value, and become indispensable to your clients.

Let me be very clear with you: process sells. You decide to do business with certain people or firms because the process they have in place tells you they are true professionals.

One of my consistent mantras is trust the process. This is actually a daily affirmation for me. What I am teaching you in this book is a process—the Value Ladder™ process. I tell all my facilitators, especially when they are in challenging moments of introspection, to trust the process. "Keep climbing," I tell them. You can always improve your process and tighten it through experience. Most important, if you have put the time and effort into your process and you've successfully implemented it with key individuals, families, or businesses, then do me and yourself a big favor and trust it!

Putting It to Work in a CPA Firm

As a CPA, what's your process? Well, you can illustrate your process in two ways for your clients: your overall client service approach and the process for a particular engagement. As an example, the elements of an exemplary client service approach might be conveyed in the following six words:

- *Partner.* You work together with clients to understand their needs and visions for the future.
- *Identify.* You determine the best services to meet clients' needs and achieve their goals.
- *Deliver.* You provide high quality services that meet clients' needs.
- *Adjust.* You revisit your original approach regularly to make necessary revisions.
- *Plan.* You keep a constant eye on long term needs and goals.
- *Communicate.* You maintain regular contact with clients to apprise them of developments that will affect them and update them on new challenges and opportunities.

Sounds good, right? It should because it's probably what you do every day for your clients. However, when you capture these steps in a process, it becomes a powerful marketing tool that gets the attention of not only potential clients but also current clients and referral sources who may not really think about the many things you do.

Although the client service process applies to every client, you also can develop a process for any particular service. Remember the CPA who talked to a golf buddy about his financial planning practice in chapter 4? Here's the process he might put together for that practice:

- *Connect.* Meet with clients to understand their needs and goals.

- *Assess.* Analyze the client's current financial situation, seeking opportunities to minimize costs, identify opportunities, and preserve and enhance wealth.
- *Map.* Create a financial plan that addresses key issues in the near and long term. Areas to consider might include college, retirement and estate planning, wealth management, family office services, and related offerings.
- *Maintain.* Update the plan based on the client's changing circumstances and new developments. Keep in regular contact to ensure that needs are met.

Now, let's think about the CPA who discussed audits with the new friend he met on the golf course. Many clients may see an audit as a troublesome process that only provides a great deal of useless detail. Here's a process that could reassure clients that you have a standard, reliable methodology that includes unexpected benefits:

- *Prepare.* We create a year-end process designed to minimize disruptions for the companies with whom we work. We provide clients with a list of dates for when we begin and end field work, mail financial statements, and meet with clients to discuss them, all in plenty of time to meet bankers' or other deadlines. (In a compilation and review, this step in the process could ensure clients that they will receive adjusting journal entries in time to close their books by their deadline.)
- *Assess.* We become familiar with the client's business and how it works.
- *Analyze.* We consider the client's processes and procedures and how well they are meeting the company's needs.
- *Report.* We share our findings in an audit report. In addition, we meet quarterly with the client to address business, tax, and other issues, using the in-depth knowledge of the company gained in the audit.
- *Review.* Each audit includes a business review that focuses on planning options that will help our clients address problems or take advantage of strategic opportunities.

- *Expand opportunities.* Through our knowledge of state, local, and federal incentives and other financing options, we help clients find more economic financing methods. We have been successful in helping clients expand their businesses or acquire other companies.
- *Lay the foundation for the future.* When necessary, we use our estate and succession planning expertise to assist clients in passing their businesses on to the next generation or a new management team.

If you think these processes sound good, imagine how great they would look illustrated in a graphic like the one from John Moshides's firm shown earlier in this chapter. What will your graphic look like? Use your imagination, considering the best way to make an impression on the clients you have and the ones you want.

Think About the Future

Now that you've considered some examples for CPA firms, think again about how you would fill out your client relationship process chart. On each of the chart's sections, go as deeply as you can. Don't neglect anything that might seem to be implied or obvious. Once you write down all the things you do for clients, you'll be surprised at the level of service you actually provide.

Once you have a formal process, understand the objectives, and can implement each step, consider another point. As you can see from the CPA examples we gave, the last step of your process should set the stage for your retention strategy and focus on a service theme. This step might include these types of actions:

- Sustaining the commitment
- Ongoing communication
- Regular meetings and communications to help meet lifetime financial or business goals
- Monitoring the client service plan
- Evaluating and reporting on the plan

This is also a good time for you to consider how to keep and grow your clients for life. What behaviors increase the probability of developing lifetime clients? For example, if a client asks what he or she should expect from you now that he or she is a valued client, he or she is, in essence, trying to understand your retention and growth process. Do you have a retention and growth process? How can you include elements of this process in the last step of your existing client relationship process?

Once you've had time to refine your client relationship process, take out your virtual screwdriver and begin tightening. It's a good idea to review your earlier Value Ladder™ answers. Does your newly developed process give you any ideas that would improve your UVP™ or business beliefs? Should you add, delete, or emphasize words or phrases in your previous steps?

How can you add more value? Can you go deeper? Place the descriptive information in your manila folders in the virtual file cabinet, and you'll find that when you refer to it—in situations you may never have dreamed of—you'll be smiling to yourself.

What's in a Name?

Now that your process is well thought out, your steps are in order, and you've come up with some ideas that would add more value, what will you call it? Your process should have a name; otherwise, it's just another generic presentation. A name leads to recognition and branding. As I have discussed, our process is called the Real Value Experience™.

Those of you who have children may remember the challenge of trying to come up with a name. Maybe you already knew what you wanted because you and your spouse were in total agreement. Or maybe the baby was in your arms and you were still trying to decide. But once you did, the name seemed absolutely perfect.

When you come to grips with your final decision, you become even more convincing and your message is even more compelling.

What are you going to call your process? You may have one overall process that applies to any service your firm offers or you may have different ones for various practice areas. How you name one or more of these processes will depend on the structure and dynamics of each firm and its client base.

The higher you climb the Value Ladder™, the closer you get to establishing a good rapport with your prospects and the more they will feel comfortable and committed to you. The more you share, the more you communicate and the closer you become. It's a great feeling. Never forget that you are the process; it's how you do what you do.

Strategic Questions to Consider

Does your organization have a formal client relationship process for a new business relationship? If yes, then

- what are the objectives of each step?
- how do you implement each step?
- what are the benefits of each step?
- what differentiates you from the competition at each step?
- have you branded or trademarked your process so it is distinctly yours?
- how well can your team communicate the process?
- why is it important that your prospects understand your process?
- what benefits can your organization realize if the team clearly communicates the process?
- how can you help your team communicate the process?

Final Thoughts

A good process will reduce uncertainty.

A process is a counterweight to the inherent uncertainty of many changes in people's lives. It is a comforting framework for any discussions about finances. Call it what you want, but prospects feel better believing that there is a strong foundation for your recommendations.

Look for linkages back to your UVP™ and business beliefs.

Great stories link one step to the next. Make sure this happens as you develop your answers.

Put it in your own words.

The best processes I've seen reflect the personality of an individual, team, or firm. They do everything possible to escape from industry jargon or overused words. Humanize it and bring in your personality.

Name it.

You've taken creative approaches to naming your kids and even your pets. Do the same for your process.

Show real value for the client.

Concentrate on articulating how each step of your process provides great value.

You're now ready to climb the Value Ladder™ to question number five, which is "Who have you done it for?"

Let's start analyzing your client successes!

Who Have You Done It For?

7

The climb up the Value Ladder™ continues as we now think about the most important people in your business life—your clients.

Giles Kavanagh, managing director of Pusateri Consulting and my key business confidant and partner for the last 10 years, always tells people that this is his favorite question on the ladder. Why? Because you really get to discuss your clients; your successes with them; and, ultimately, the real value that you have provided. Giles always challenges participants with penetrating questions about how well they know their clients. "Did you really connect with their key emotion?" he asks. "What is keeping them up at night? What did you do for them? How has this translated into real value?" Our clients continually raise their AHA cards as they listen to success stories.

More than ever, today, you must listen to what clients are telling you in order to analyze their issues, understand their emotions, and provide solutions. Here is what they are saying:

- I am more informed.
- I have greater choices.
- I am more enlightened.
- I want to know what I am getting for my money.
- I am less swayed by marketing gimmickry.
- I am more selective.
- I have more options for professional services. Some of these options are less costly than you. So, you better be prepared to explain to me the value that you provide and why it's priced the way it's priced.

Big gulp. Here we go again!

You and I also are among this changing group. Look in your own mirror again and reflect on the changes in your life. It probably amazes you to think about your life continuum and the key events that have affected your personal and professional life.

This chapter will help you be more introspective, looking at your relationships with those key people who help pay your bills and allow you to live the life you lead. Those special people are called clients. I want you to really think about them and take the time to evaluate the success you have had with them. Because when you are able to speak about your client relationships knowledgeably and with confidence, you will have a better story to tell potential clients who are considering handing over more business to you.

To get started, think about what you have accomplished, picking your own appropriate time frame. What kind of success have you had in the last year, this decade, or since you started in the profession? You will probably surprise yourself when you do this exercise. You can do it from an individual or organizational perspective. A senior leader from one of my major clients was actually blown away by listening to his leadership team describe the things they were proud of. These were leaders opening up their hearts and pointing to things that other participants had taken for granted. Eighteen members of this leadership team developed a list of over 60 accomplishments. I didn't think the exercise was ever going to end. I knew how valuable the discussion was when this valued client said, "Why didn't we start the program here?" It was that powerful. Those 60+ items were eventually categorized into 6 areas. The leadership team stood a little taller and exuded an aura of confidence that I had not observed before. The same can happen to you or your firm. What you will find is that many of the successes will be a key component in the answer to the next question on the Value Ladder™, which is, "What makes you different?" More on that later.

Another story is worth mentioning from a recent client workshop that I led. The managing partner of a successful regional financial services firm asked if I would be interested in coaching his team. He wanted to know

- what I would do first.
- where I would focus.
- what he could expect from my work.
- what is my process.

Doesn't this sound familiar? Remember reading about similar questions in the previous chapters?

We were riding in a golf cart before the company's golf outing and I said, "Tell me about your clients. Who is your ideal client? Who really pumps you up? Who do you enjoy working with the most? Who really appreciates your value? Who are you proud to say is your client? Who gives you goose bumps when you talk about them to others? Who, if you could multiply this client by 100, would give you the ultimate client base for your practice? Describe this client to me and tell me about the success you've had with that client."

Do you know the answers to these questions? Most CPAs probably could come up with some decent responses, but they may never have done the kind of analysis necessary to hone in on the most valuable insights. That means they are taking a passive approach to client selection by letting the client pick them instead of targeting the individuals and businesses that are really best for their firms. They are probably unaware of the strengths that draw and hold certain kinds of clients.

You see, I'm from the school that teaches us to create our own future. I've even developed hypothetical classes and theoretical degrees for myself, such as my Introduction to Clients course, which focused on the question, "Who do you want to have as your clients?" My self-styled MBA in Advanced Client Relationships taught me about going narrow and deep with my focus. My thesis on client success focused on creating a culture of lifetime clients. Key doctoral coursework in my Personal University emphasized alignment of my values with my clients' values, the understanding of lifetime value, and the real meaning of growth and retention of these clients. It also taught me the benefit of obtaining referrals without ever having to ask for them (contrary to current referral gurus' thinking today) and the constant quest for the answers to the ultimate introspective client questions.

Telling the Story

Translating what you do into meaningful terms for your prospects and clients is best achieved by sharing how you have added value to meet your clients' unique needs. Who you do business with is, of course, a private matter between you and your clients. You don't want to share the specifics of a client's personal situation, but you can still use successes with former and current clients to your advantage. You can go into your virtual file cabinet and pull out the stories you need, when appropriate.

You also can describe your clients to a prospect by focusing on the market segments you serve, like businesses in a certain size segment or industry, high net worth individuals, corporate executives, physicians, or not-for-profit organizations. That way, you do not divulge any confidential information, and your current client relationships are protected. You will come across as professional, and you will be able to describe the kinds of people and businesses who want to work with you and the solutions you have found for them.

Tools to Help You Analyze Your Clients and Markets

Here's what the fifth step on the Value Ladder™ does for you: it forces you to perform a deeper analysis of your clients and to think about who they are and whether your interests are aligned with theirs. It asks you to decide with which new clients you would like to work. Do your current clients appreciate your value and process? Are they willing to pay you for it? This exercise also will force you to think about whether you want to continue working with certain clients, as well. The result is a better sense of who you should be serving and a heightened ability to articulate the value you bring to clients.

I have two great tools, among others, in my *Discovering Your Value* workbook that I'd like to share with you. The first is a chart called the "Individual Client Analysis." Here, you can break your analysis down into the following four key elements:

1. Who are your individual clients?
2. What are their key emotional issues?
3. What are the solutions for these issues?
4. What is the real value you provide?

The second chart is called the "Market Segment Analysis." One focuses on individual clients, and the other covers specific target markets.

This is a great exercise for you. Take some time and write down the names of your top clients in the first column on the client chart and some of your target markets in the first column of your market chart.

Individual Client Analysis

1: INDIVIDUAL CLIENTS	2: KEY EMOTIONAL ISSUES *Challenges—Circumstances* *Concerns—Frustrations* *Opportunities—Needs* *Problems*	3: SOLUTIONS	4: REAL VALUE

Market Segment Analysis

1: CLIENTS	2: KEY EMOTIONAL ISSUES *Challenges—Circumstances* *Concerns—Frustrations* *Opportunities—Needs* *Problems*	3: SOLUTIONS	4: REAL VALUE

The second column (on both charts), Key Emotional Issues, is very important to study. Why? Because, as I've said, the best way to learn how to sell is to first understand what it is like to buy. How well do you really understand your clients' emotions? Your clients and prospects each have various challenges, circumstances, concerns, frustrations, opportunities, needs, and problems. We call these the seven key emotional issues. This column forces you to think about how well you know your clients and markets. What key emotions have you addressed lately?

I also refer to these emotional issues as driving and restraining forces. *Driving forces* are positive factors that lead or drive you toward attaining business and personal goals. *Restraining forces* are negative factors that could potentially hold you back from achieving your big picture goals. It's critical to understand the driving and restraining forces affecting your clients because the more you can relate to your clients' emotions, the better you can emotionally connect with them.

The Key Emotional Issues

Here is a complete listing of the seven key emotional issues with examples of what your business or individual clients might be saying:

1. *Challenges.* Things that inhibit the client from achieving goals. Example: "An uncertain economy and the loss of some big customers have prevented us from meeting our growth targets. I'm not even sure we can maintain our current sales levels."

2. *Circumstances.* A situation that accompanies an event. Example: "I had to take a lower paying job after a downsizing, and I'm no longer sure we can pay for my son's college tuition."

3. *Concerns.* Issues of interest or importance. Example: "My wife may have to quit her job because of her father's serious illness."

4. *Frustrations.* Issues causing the client to feel disappointed or unfulfilled. Example: "We just never seem to get ahead. Something is always holding us back"

5. *Needs.* What the client wants or requires. Example: "Our children will be entering college over the next two years. We need funds for tuition and maybe for Dad's care."

6. *Opportunities.* Situations favorable to the attainment of a goal. Example: "We finally landed that big client we've been working to win."

7. *Problems.* Questions raised out of concern or doubt. Example: "Should we cancel our expansion plans because of the troubled economy?"

The best way to understand your clients' emotions is to first understand your own.

For example, maybe one of your challenges is that you are so busy managing the growth of your practice that you don't have time to bring in new business or institute needed administrative changes that would translate into a more efficient and profitable firm.

I've offered some examples. Now, what are some of your emotional issues?

Remember, understanding your own emotions first tends to improve your empathetic listening skills. Instead of just "hearing" your prospects, you actually "listen" better. You acknowledge your clients with respect because you know what they're experiencing, and your connection to them strengthens dramatically.

Try the exercise for yourself. List your own seven key emotional issues. Then, think of some of your top clients to determine how well you've emotionally connected to them. Surely, they have their own challenges, circumstances, concerns, frustrations, needs, opportunities, and problems. Do you know what they are? Do your clients know how you can help address them? Are you as successful at making an emotional connection as you thought you were?

You really need to take the time to talk and listen to your clients. Some CPAs are so busy performing client services that they don't get to know their clients or their key emotional issues, but this step is a critical aspect of client analysis.

Delivering Solutions

All right, let's say you've listed all of the issues your prospects and clients may be dealing with. It's time to deliver solutions (column three). (Make sure you look at both charts and analyze both clients and markets.) The solutions could be, say, personal financial or estate planning for individual clients or business planning or a host of other services for companies.

When you start concentrating on solutions, then you also begin thinking in a more comprehensive, consultative way instead of simply delivering a service. You're also mindful of being a problem solver for your clients, which would be another value added component in your differentiation from the competition.

Don't forget all that work you've done defining the uniqueness of your solutions in the Unique Value Proposition™ (UVP™) exercise. Is the work I challenged you to do in question number two of the Value Ladder™ ("What do you do?") connecting here, as well? It should be. Are your solutions truly comprehensive? Are they integrated, personalized, and customized? Get the picture?

The more you work on these concepts, the more they transform from threads of information into a tightrope, a rope that is strong, built on conviction and integrity, and representative of the most important thing you have to offer—you.

Continuing on, column four of the chart is Real Value. What is your real value? We'll explain this concept in more depth when we cover question seven on our Value Ladder™. For now, think about your clients, their emotions, and the issues they are struggling with and the solutions you are providing. When you eventually reach that seventh step, you'll have more insight into the value you provide your clients and prospects, and you'll be better equipped to fill out the Real Value area.

Impressing a Prospect

Think about a potential client who could significantly raise your profile or revenue. The one who could make a major impact on your business or career. The one you really covet. The one you would be proud to say is a client. Write down the name of this person or company.

Now, if your prospect were to ask you for a reference, to which clients would you send him or her? What questions about you and your firm do you think your prospect might ask your key clients?

If I were to pick up the phone and call some of your top clients, I would ask them the following key questions:

1. How long have you been working with this CPA?
2. Who else did you consider?
3. How did you make your decision?
4. Why did you decide to do business with him or her?
5. What, specifically, is he or she doing for you?
6. What do you value most about your CPA?
7. What is the real value that your CPA provides? What contribution has he or she made to you or your company's financial well being?

Imagine filling out a form like this summarizing some of the answers. Do you think it might give you some perspective on your clients' thoughts? I do. When you learn how to ask these questions of your own clients in a relaxed manner, you'll be amazed at the power of this communication technique.

Key Clients	Why Did You Decide to Do Business With ...?	How Would You Describe What They Do for You ...?	What Do You Value Most About ...?	What Is the Real Value That ... Has Provided to You?

Often, clients will answer that they have connected with you emotionally and intellectually. They feel that you "get" them and their problems, concerns, and dreams. That's what you want to hear. You can never do too much introspection on your relationship with key clients. Existing clients are the core of your future growth opportunities, especially your "A" clients. Always remember that it is a lot easier to keep and grow an existing valued client than it is to prospect for another one.

Acres of Diamonds

This is my all-time favorite story about the concept of client success. The late Earl Nightingale, the world-renowned success motivation guru, eloquently told the "Acres of Diamonds" story on the Nightingale-Conant *Lead the Field* audiotape series. This brilliant true story says it better than anything I've ever heard. Here is a transcript:

> An African farmer had heard tales about the other farmers who had made millions by discovering diamond mines. These tales so excited the farmer that he could hardly wait to sell his farm and go prospecting for diamonds himself. So he sold the farm and spent the rest of his life wandering the African continent, searching unsuccessfully for the gleaming gems that brought such high prices on the markets of the world. Finally, worn out and in a fit of despondency, he threw himself into a river and drowned.

> Meanwhile, back at the ranch, or farm, in this case, the man who had bought the farm happened to be crossing the small stream on the property. Suddenly, there was a bright flash of blue and red light from the stream's bottom. He bent down, picked up the stone—it was a good-sized stone—and, admiring it, later put it on his fireplace mantel as an interesting curiosity.

Several weeks later, a visitor to his home picked up the stone, looked closely at it, hefted it in his hand—and nearly fainted. He asked the farmer if he knew what he'd found. When the farmer said no, that he'd thought it was a piece of crystal, the visitor told him he had found one of the largest diamonds ever discovered. The farmer had trouble believing that. He told the man that his creek was full of such stones—not as large, perhaps, as the one on the mantel, but they were sprinkled generously throughout the creek bottom.

Needless to say, the farm the first farmer had sold so that he might find a diamond mine turned out to be the most productive diamond mine on the entire African continent. The first farmer had owned, free and clear, acres of diamonds, but had sold them for practically nothing in order to look for them elsewhere.

The moral is clear: If only the first farmer had taken the time to study and prepare himself—to learn what diamonds looked like in their rough state—and, since he had already owned a piece of the African continent, to thoroughly explore the property he had before looking for elsewhere, all of his wildest dreams would have come true.

Clients for a Lifetime

What struck me so profoundly about this story was the idea that we are all standing in the middle of our own acres of diamonds. If we have the wisdom and patience to effectively and intelligently explore the work in which we are now engaged and to explore ourselves, we can usually find the riches we seek.

I've developed my own acres of diamonds exercise to help you evaluate your client successes. This will help you gain a greater understanding of how well you know your clients. It also will give you greater clarity on the success you are having with each client. I suggest you start with your top 10 clients and then extend it to your top 25; then top 50; then, ultimately, your top 100. Rank them based on the revenue you earn from providing professional services. I prefer this approach for ranking purposes, but you can go deeper and do a more thorough profitability analysis. Remember, the deeper you can go, the better for analyzing client successes.

Clients	Services You Provide	Revenue $ You Are Paid	Estimated Lifetime Value	Long Term Plan for Client	Banker	Attorney	Referrals	How Would They Describe My Value?
1.								
2.								
3.								
4.								
5.								
6.								
7.								
8.								
9.								
10.								

Next, list the services you provide followed by the exact revenue dollars this client provides.

The next column—estimated lifetime value (ELV)—is unbelievably revealing. This column represents one of those great AHAs as the light bulbs get even brighter. To illustrate this concept in my presentations, I usually choose an audience member whom I guess will probably have a long career ahead of him or her. I say, "How long will you be in this business, Ryan? Twenty-five years? Great! Let's assume your client is Mr. Ideal. You are getting $10,000 in fees from this client annually. Are you with me so far?

"Okay, what will Mr. Ideal be worth to you over the next 25 years?" Gulp. Sweaty palms.

"Well," says Ryan, "25 years × $10,000 is $250,000."

I say, "No, not exactly, Ryan. You aren't considering the growth opportunities that might make this client worth much more to you. So, how else can Mr. Ideal grow with you? Give me one way. Expanding your current services? Maybe you can begin to do personal financial planning for the company owners or offer some value added services. Maybe someone will say to you, 'Gee, I didn't even know you guys did this. Why didn't you even talk to me about this before?'" Next to winging it, letting added client business slip through your fingers is the second most dreaded disease in the business of selling or consulting.

"How about referrals?" Good, that's two. Ryan says, "That's it, I guess."

Then I say, "No, Ryan, there's one more. With an improved UVP™ supported by tight business beliefs and a unique and comprehensive process, you may, in fact, consider raising your fees at some point. Your new message of value should be greatly appreciated by your clients, which means they'll be willing to pay more."

Then, I add, "You'll realize that pricing your value can only be accomplished if you know your value. So, Ryan, back to Mr. Ideal. What's he really worth? Twenty-five more years in the business; over $10,000 per year in revenues; and add on the 3 AHAs of estimated lifetime value. What do you have?" (Bigger gulp. Sweat all over your body.) "Mr. Ideal may be worth 7 figures to your firm over the next 25 years."

AHA!

So, to conclude, I say to him, "Ryan, do you understand which new services Mr. Ideal may need? Have you talked to him about his own personal financial situation? Do you know his bankers and attorneys? Are they aware of the value you offer to your mutual client?" When you begin to think this way, you're on the road to expanding your clients' ELV.

Give this exercise an honest appraisal. Do it by yourself then bring your team together. You'll be amazed at your answers, and I guarantee that your honest dialogue regarding this and the next Value Ladder™ steps will be some of the most important time you will ever invest in your business.

Shouldn't You?: Thinking About What You're Missing

A point of reference for the acres of diamonds exercise:

What are your opportunities for revenue growth with your clients? Might you be leaving some dollars on the table?

1. *New business.* Do your clients know everything you can do for businesses and individuals? Many CPAs regularly look for chances to expand their services to existing clients. Shouldn't you?
2. *Referrals.* Many CPAs tell their clients that they are seeking new business and ask them for the names of potential prospects. Shouldn't you?
3. *Intergenerational wealth transference.* Whether working with wealthy individuals or family businesses, many CPAs proactively assess family opportunities that might provide more service potential. Shouldn't you?
4. *Higher fees.* Many CPAs actively reposition themselves; their value; and, consequently, their pricing. Shouldn't you?

Strategic Questions to Consider

We began this chapter by considering what a prospect would want to know about your current clients. To answer his or her questions, you need to answer some of your own, including the following:

- Who are my clients?
- How many clients do I have?
- Are my clients' priorities changing?
- Who should be my clients?
- Do I have a specialization strategy?
- Does it make sense for my marketplace?
- How am I currently adding value to my clients?
- How would my clients measure my success?
- How can I become my clients' one and only trusted business advisor?
- Are there good ways for me to educate prospects on current client successes?

Answering these questions allows you to focus on the client. You will consider who they are, who they should be, their priorities, and how their priorities are changing. It will force you to think about your specializations and whether they are well-suited to your current client base. Your introspection also will help you focus on how your clients will measure your success.

With all of this in mind, you should understand who your coveted clients are and, more important, recognize the successes you have had with them. Only then can you begin to share the answers to, "Who have you done it for?" with confidence, passion, and speed.

Remember to revisit your virtual file cabinet. You should be ready to reach for the fifth drawer with folders labeled "Your Potential Clients" and "Existing Clients," which will hold appropriate stories that outline your client successes. Can you see your file cabinet expanding?

Final Thoughts

How well do you really know your clients?

Don't ever take for granted these people called clients. Always remember the following great introspective question: are you convinced that your clients are convinced that you are adding value? You can never do too much introspection on your relationship with key clients.

Know your clients' emotions as if they were your own.

I always laugh when I watch a *Seinfeld* episode and see Kramer doing one of his patented crazy moves. He reacts to those around him, and they sure know how he feels. When an emotion is shared, it should be like a doorbell going off or a phone ringing. It makes a connection. So, open the door or pick up the phone. Be like Kramer.

Get comfortable asking clients key questions about you, your firm, your work, and your value.

No better source exists than the people who receive your work—your clients. Take a deep breath and ask. Get ready to zip it up and just listen to what they tell you. You will probably be pleasantly surprised.

Do the acres of diamonds chart.

Another wake-up call awaits you. If you want to assess how well you really know your clients, try this exercise on for size.

Now, let's move on to the next question, which is "What makes you different?"

Time to learn about your umbrella of distinction.

What Makes You Different? 8

"So, Leo, what makes you different?" I am often asked this question when I give a presentation. It can come off as a challenge, but I don't mind because I believe people have every right to ask if they are considering investing time and money to attend one of my programs. I usually can't wait to answer.

"Thank you for asking me the question," I say. "I can distinguish myself in three ways. One, through my company versus other competitive alternatives. Two, with my solutions versus other options. Three, and most important, through my personal level of differentiation. It's what I stand for. It's my set of core values. It's what you can expect from working with me."

I continue, "Where would you like me to focus? My company, my solutions, or what I stand for? Better yet, another way to answer that question—I specialize in helping other committed professionals like you answer the very same question. What makes me different? I help you increase your confidence, passion, and speed. Where would you like me to focus?" I ask.

Perhaps you've encountered a similar situation. Have you ever been directly challenged? When I ask people in my workshops what makes them different, I usually get some nervous laughter. So I ask the group, "Well, tell me, what other ways can this question be asked?"

People respond by saying, "My prospect will say he's talking to another firm and will ask how my firm compares." People also will say, "Another firm told my prospect that they have very deep financial planning expertise. My prospect wants to know if I can match it." Another possible response is, "What can I expect from working with you as an individual? What are your standards? What will you bring to the table?"

Setting Yourself Apart

After honest introspection, if you can distinguish yourself at a world-class level, well, that's half the battle. But most CPAs I speak to say they need help in talking about what sets them apart. They don't know enough about their competition, and they want to be able to fluently discuss their differentiation.

You should be conversationally proficient regarding your core, or direct, competitors and their solutions. Put yourself in the consumer's shoes. You are now the consumer or, better yet, the client looking for change. How would you feel in these scenarios:

- You are shopping for a new BMW and stop by a Mercedes dealer. You ask questions about the differences in the two cars. You get vague answers to your questions because the salesperson knows very little about the BMW you are in love with. How do you feel about that?
- You are evaluating custom homebuilders and one of them just can't agree with your dream architectural plans. Another one understands your vision, sits down with you, and works together to create a plan that is architecturally sound; within budget; and, ultimately, becomes the home of your dreams. How does this make you feel?
- You are checking out two local establishments to determine which one will host an event for clients. One location understands what you mean by Four Seasons-type service, and they can demonstrate it to you. The other establishment says simply, "Don't worry, we will help you pull it off." How do you feel about that?

What happens when your clients ask a big question but disguise it as a simple one, such as, "What makes you different?" Does your response lack the details they are really interested in hearing? Some CPAs say their prospects don't ask this question, but they know their prospects are thinking and wondering about it, even if they are not asking outright.

The first thing you need to do when your prospect asks what makes you different is to qualify that question. Ask, "Different from whom, different from what?" Tell your prospect you need to better understand what he or she means so you can give him or her the answer he or she is seeking. Does your prospect mean different from another organization, different in terms of solutions, or different as an individual? Does your prospect want to know what he or she can expect from you in a partnership? You also can assure your prospect that you know the most important decision he or she will make is whether he or she is comfortable with you and your team.

By asking your prospect to clarify the question, "Different from what?" or by using a respectful phrase like, "Help me to help you," you will be able to focus your answers on the specific differentiation factors the prospect is considering. Your response to the prospect's questions will let him or her know the breadth and depth of your differentiation knowledge and will set you apart.

Remember, always be in the moment. If your client asks the question when you're talking about a certain competitor, clearly, your answer will focus on that competitor. Use your good judgment. If you begin rambling, your intuition will tell you that you need to further clarify and confirm the question.

CPAs will ask me, "Isn't my Unique Value Proposition™ (UVP™) a good enough statement of what makes me different?" Well, no. Your UVP™ is your proposal of value to someone. You develop it to the degree that it does, in fact, distinguish you, but at some point, more questions will come up about your work. At some point, a prospect might want to know how your UVP™, or how clients' experience with your UVP™, is actually different from a competitive alternative.

It's inevitable that the deeper you go into the dialogue and the higher you climb the Value Ladder™, the more you will have to distinguish yourself. This is especially true as your prospect gets closer to deciding to give you a significant engagement and to partner with you for the long term. The more critically a prospect analyzes you, the more proficient you need to be at distinguishing yourself.

Sometimes, your prospect might jump from, "How do you do what you do?" right into the question, "What makes you different?" This often happens because your process will become your solution. You'll see how the questions on the Value Ladder™ tend to build on each other, complement each other, and inspire deeper consideration. This creates a perfect opportunity to go into your virtual file cabinet and pull out the appropriate answers.

Your file drawers should contain virtual manila folders with information on your core competitors so you also can quickly distinguish yourself at an organizational level. Within those competitor folders, you might have additional information on their solutions. You also may have manila folders containing each of your core values, those ultimate levels of distinction that focus on what you truly stand for.

Three Ways to Distinguish Yourself (or, Bring Your Umbrella to the Party)

After I broke down the elements of the question, "What makes you different?" early on in the development of the Value Ladder™, I realized there were three key ways to distinguish myself. Keep these three points in mind:

- You must distinguish your firm in relation to the competition. This is called *organizational differentiation*.
- You must distinguish your firm's solutions. This is called *solution differentiation*.
- You must distinguish yourself on an individual or team level. This is called *individual or team differentiation*.

During one of my training sessions, I presented these three levels in a great visualization as an umbrella.

When you press the button on a folding umbrella, it pops open, right? The top of the open umbrella represents your company. All of the metal spokes holding up the umbrella represent the solutions you provide. At this spokes level, you should be looking at your integrated solutions, which are the products, services, or programs you provide to your prospects and clients.

Consider a top CPA firm that won a lucrative accounting and tax client. It did this by emphasizing not simply the compliance services the firm would handle but also expressly detailing how the information the firm would provide could help the client cut costs and streamline procedures. The firm demonstrated an understanding of the client's industry and explained how it could provide solutions to the issues the company faced. The firm highlighted all of the spokes (the solutions) under the firm umbrella and demonstrated that it could provide unique value to the client in a seamless and cohesive manner. This firm distinguished itself.

What Makes You Different?
Differentiate yourself in three ways:

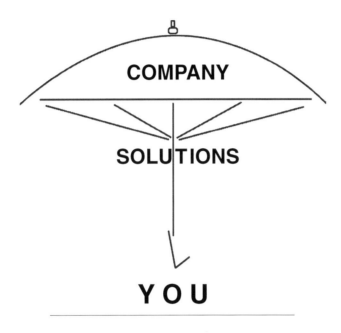

The last part of the umbrella, but certainly not the least, is the person or team holding it up. It's the most important person for you to distinguish, the man or woman of the hour—you. What do you stand for? What can a client expect from working with you? What are your standards? What is your code of ethics? What are your values?

We will spend appropriate time here developing answers to these questions because I truly believe this is the greatest way to distinguish yourself. The key point is how well can you distinguish your umbrella?

We'll explore that now by looking at all of the elements, including your company, your solutions, and you.

Who Are Your Real Competitors?

I'm often told when I conduct sessions that I shouldn't spend much time talking about what makes my client's firm different from the competition.

It often doesn't crystallize for clients until we do a follow-up program that understanding the competition is, in fact, very important when it comes to differentiating yourself. At the next session, I ask the leaders questions such as, "What makes you different from XYZ & Company?" That's when the firm leaders see their talented staff members fumbling for answers.

CPAs need the language to answer this question with confidence. In 9 out of 10 cases, people will tell me that discussing the competition is a good dialogue to have within the firm because they need insights into the competition when talking to potential clients. Unless they attend a session like mine, however, firm leaders and staff will seldom actually discuss the issue. Sometimes, the top leaders think that the staff already know all about the competition; in many cases, the partners themselves may not have even given a lot of thought to their competitors. If they have, they probably have not communicated their knowledge well to the staff or given them opportunities to understand how competition works and what it means to their firm.

Before you can answer all the questions about what makes you different from other firms, you of course need to know who they are and a little bit about them. If you work with high net worth individuals, for instance, your competition might not only be other CPA firms that offer this service but also non-CPA wealth managers or private banking professionals. If you know of other professionals managing money or providing other services to your clients, then they are also competitors and should be considered in your competitive analysis.

Just how much do you need to know about your competition? Enough to be conversationally proficient. In other words, you need to be able to look at your prospects when they ask you any questions about any of your core competitors and answer with such expertise that they will say to themselves, "This person really knows the business. She understands competitive options. I am dealing with a professional."

It's very important to speak respectfully about your core competitors. Never utter a negative word. You should be able to educate an interested prospect and tell him or her more than anyone else, informing him or her about the competitive alternatives just by sharing your knowledge. Doing that alone—being that well-informed and competent—immediately sets you apart, all other factors being equal.

You should do enough analysis to be knowledgeable, of course, but not so much that you paralyze yourself into worrying about how you stack up. Remember, the most important thing is to be an expert in discussing your own firm, your solutions, and yourself first. Let's get started thinking about your own umbrella now.

Organizational Differentiation

Even if you are creating an individual, rather than an organizational, Value Ladder™, it's a good idea to know about the competition. To begin, give yourself this simple quiz:

- What are the main competitive differences between your two top CPA firm competitors in your own market?
- How is the law firm you work with different from another legal entity in your town?
- How is the bank you do business with different from any other in your city?

Makes you stop and think, doesn't it? When it comes to considering your own law firm or bank, you probably have many reasons for choosing a professional services firm or financial services option, but you might not have ever articulated them. Now, put yourself in your clients' shoes and begin to think about what makes you different.

The most important question is how your firm differs from whomever your prospect is asking about at the moment. Always remember that if your potential client is getting accounting or consulting services anywhere else, these firms are competitors, and they can encroach upon your business.

Key Competitive Differentiation Concepts

One great way to assess organizational differentiation (which also applies to solution differentiation) is to consider the following concepts as you position your strategy:

- *The concept of uniqueness.* As defined in chapter 4 on developing your UVP™, *unique* means exclusive, matchless, or one-of-a-kind. What characteristics make you or your firm truly unique? If you are doing this at the organizational level, sit down with your team, whether it's the management group or the entire firm. I'm sure you'll be able to develop a long list of traits that set you apart. In fact, the more firm members you include, the better perspective you will gain. Many of your administrative people may have great stories about excellent examples of client service that partners know nothing about. If you're doing this as an individual, you can think about what makes you unique, as well as what unique aspects of your firm further set you apart. What's important here, though, are the things that you or your firm do that nobody else can offer.
- *The concept of competitive advantages.* This one really gets you thinking. Are you truly better than your competition in ways that are important to your potential client? If so, then that's a competitive advantage, something that you should definitely emphasize in your presentations to prospects and in your strategic plan.
- *The concept of parity.* In an increasingly commoditized world, we can try our best to distinguish ourselves, but sometimes, things seem so similar that they look and feel to be a competitive "wash."

  We have a lot of fun in our programs proving this point. I bring a bag of peanuts to a session and pass one out to each participant. "Don't eat it," is my first command. "Let's have some fun." And we always do. "Do you all agree that some clients see our services as commodities?" They all agree. "Why the peanut in a shell," I ask. "Because they, like you, look the same. If they could talk, they would talk the same, walk the same, and smell the same. Well, let's prove the point wrong." I then instruct the attendees to write down as many characteristics as they can about the peanut in their hand. Ready? Set? Go! Watching sophisticated professionals doing this is a hoot.

I ask participants, "What did you write down? Yell it out!"

"Mine is dented," says one. "Mine has two peanuts in the shell," says another. "Mine has a crack in it," says yet another. The attendees have fun getting outside of their box.

I then say, "Now that you've heard what your peers have said, find one more characteristic. Go deeper and have some more fun." More crazy answers follow. If the group is small, I collect all the peanuts. I throw them on a table and say, "Okay, come and claim your peanut now." Lots of laughter and good-natured kidding takes place. This great exercise really illustrates that we can find unique attributes if we look hard enough. Invariably, some people cannot find their peanuts. And, yes, this can make competitive people very upset!

Then I ask them, "How does studying a commodity relate to your challenges in distinguishing your firm and yourself?" Usually, participants will have the following responses:

- "I didn't study what was in front of me well enough."
- "I took a short cut.
- "I need to pay closer attention to details. There really are differences if you look hard enough."

What we learn from this exercise is that we are different and we are unique. Even though we may look the same, given some thought, we can distinguish ourselves. Another observation I heard from an attendee seemed to sum it up. "You need to pay attention to details. Differentiation is in the eye of the beholder." Can you imagine the challenge your clients must have? Look at this chart. You may have a lot of work ahead to distinguish yourself!

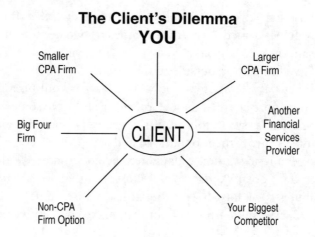

The Client's Dilemma
YOU

Smaller CPA Firm

Larger CPA Firm

Big Four Firm

Another Financial Services Provider

CLIENT

Non-CPA Firm Option

Your Biggest Competitor

That's right, my friends, some of you do look the same, talk the same, and smell the same. Are you starting to visualize what I'm talking about here?

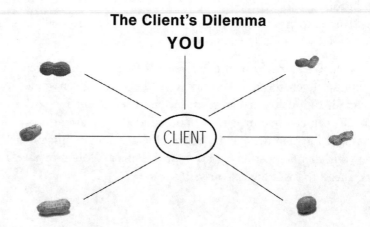

The Client's Dilemma
YOU

CLIENT

- *The concept of competitive disadvantages.* The opposite of competitive advantages, this is what your competitors truly do better than you. Honest introspection helps here because it forces you to go deeper into the analysis of your own uniqueness and competitive advantages. Though difficult at times, the process makes you ultimately better and more confident by helping you identify your strengths and promote them and, just as important, target your weaknesses and address them.
- *The concept of competitors' uniqueness.* Here's an important point to remember: your competitors believe they are unique, too. What makes them unique in their own estimation? What do they tell their prospective clients about themselves—the same prospective clients that you're pursuing? You should know. I'd rather be playing cards knowing what's in my opponents' hands, wouldn't you? I can then strategize differently and make the most effective use of my resources. You can, too.

Organization Differentiation

Take a look at the following table:

1: Key Competitors	2: Your Organization's Uniqueness	3: Your Competitive Advantages	4: Parity	5: Your Competitor's Competitive Advantages	6: Your Competitor's Uniqueness
1.					
2.					
3.					
4.					
5.					

- In column one, identify your top five competitors.
- In column two, identify your organization's unique attributes.
- In column three, identify your own competitive advantages.
- In column four, identify the characteristics of your firm and your competitor's firms that you feel are fairly equal.
- In column five, identify your competitor's advantages.
- In column six, identify your competitor's unique aspects.

Fill in as much as you can. You'll begin to get the language down, and the strategic words will come. You'll start sounding like a champion.

You may come away with a powerful statement, such as the following:

- "Our firm has an unmatched approach to financial planning."
- "Based on our extensive analysis of the marketplace, we truly believe we present many competitive advantages."

Not bad, huh? Sounds pretty good in actual dialogue, especially after you've done the hard work of analyzing your story.

Solution Differentiation

You may know what businesses you're competing against, but what do they actually offer? Shouldn't you know? Won't it make it easier to position yourself in a crowded market?

1: Solutions Against Which You Directly Compete	2: Your Solutions' Uniqueness	3: Your Solutions' Advantages	4: Parity	5: Your Competitor's Advantages	6: Your Competitor's Uniqueness
1.					
2.					
3.					
4.					
5.					

Take a look again at the spokes holding up the umbrella—your solutions. Maybe some of your solutions are a full range of services, personal and customized service and expertise in specific areas.

If I speak to a product expert at a consumer products company, I expect him or her to educate me not only on his or her product concentration, but also on key competitors. Through your contacts in the business community and what you hear from clients and staff members who have worked for other firms, you should be able to get a similar sense of what the competition, and their solutions, are like.

What Do You Stand For?

This is the most important concept on your umbrella level of distinction: What do you stand for? What are your values?

Can you think of an organization that lives its values? What organization, company, or team comes to mind? You know what traits I'm talking about: measurable quality, impeccable service, top-notch in everything they do. When participants share their responses with me, you can hear the passion in their voices as they relate their experiences.

I love this part of our program because participants are ready to jump out of their chairs, and sometimes, they almost sound like they work for a favorite organization. They are apostles, passionate advocates, and significant referrers. "Tell me about your experiences with these companies," I ask. "What value do they provide to the marketplace? If I called your top clients, could they list you or your team or your company as one of these organizations? Would they be raving fans? Do they have you in their personal hall of fame?"

Isn't that your goal? I know it's mine.

Distinguish Yourself

Many companies develop broad-based core values that are called mission statements, value statements, or their beliefs or principles. I'll ask a company representative, "What are your core values?" He or she will state a belief in taking care of the client first or customizing solutions for clients. Sometimes, when I hear these things, or see them posted in the office, I feel these words are meaningless. Is this just something that the company hired a consultant to put together or is the company really living it?

Another fun and rewarding moment during our retreats is when we ask seminar attendees, after spending two days with each other, to use key words to describe their fellow participants. It's amazing the perceptions we formulate about each other in such a short period of time. Think about the opinions you form about the people and organizations with which you are considering doing business. Now, imagine the perceptions your prospects develop about you in a short period. Do others believe you are living your values?

This is what I call the individual or team differentiation. If you were asked by your prospect to distinguish yourself as an individual from a competitor, what would you say? Would you say what you stand for?

What are your core values? Your code of ethics? If you bring up your ethics or values, use descriptive words that you really believe in your heart describe what clients can expect from you, your team, or your organization.

Always remember that business is first a meeting of the hearts then it becomes a meeting of the minds. If the most important thing you have to distinguish is you, then the best way to distinguish yourself is by speaking from your heart and connecting with someone else through sharing your standards, code of ethics, and core values. It is imperative you have this stuff down pat.

If you really haven't thought too much about your core values, you might want to begin by analyzing them. Are your values internally or externally focused? Are they company values or individual values or are they possibly one and the same? To get you started in thinking about your values, here are some words you might find yourself using to describe them. We've mixed in verbs, nouns, and adjectives, so you can use them as needed in your considerations:

VALUE LEXICON

Abide	Gracious	Patience
Ability	Genuine	Perceptive
Accountable	Heartfelt	Pragmatic
Affable	Honesty	Professional
Balanced	Honorable	Rational
Caring	Independent	Reasonable
Commitment	Innovative	Reliable
Competent	Insightful	Respect
Conscientious	Integrity	Safety
Conversationalist	Intelligent	Serious
Dedicated	Judicious	Sincere
Dependable	Kind	Thoughtful
Education	Love	Trust
Enthusiasm	Loyalty	Value
Expert	Objective	Warm
Fairness	Open	Well-rounded
Forthright	Organized	Wholehearted
Friendliness	Partner	Wise
Fun	Passion	

The most important element of differentiation is literally the person with whom the prospect partners. Even though you can distinguish your company and solutions, the critical component is you. You are the company, process, and value.

So, what do you stand for?

Opening Your Umbrella

I love the game of golf. Due to our challenging climate, I have a golf umbrella on my golf bag. An umbrella, of course, is used to protect you and your clothing from the rain. Your umbrella of distinction is used in the same way—to protect you from the danger of getting lost in the crowd. Use it when you need it.

When the conditions warrant, you take the umbrella off your bag and open it. You will feel better protected. Your umbrella of distinction sits in the sixth drawer of your virtual file cabinet. Open your "Organizational Differentiation" manila folder. Maybe you have files on your key competitors. I do. Maybe you have a manila folder on your solutions or your competitor's solutions. I do. Maybe you have files on what you stand for. I do.

Differentiation 3x5

You can use the work you do on this step of the Value Ladder™ to create a powerful graphic depiction of what sets you apart. Begin by filling in the following chart. This chart goes everywhere with me. I can't even begin to tell you how important this is. It is your complete summary for your differentiation answer. It has won my firm numerous client mandates over the years, and it can do the same for you and your firm. The beauty of the chart is that it gathers intelligence from the previous chapter on client successes. Remember the exercise in which you thought about successes that you are proud of from a firm perspective? It all comes home here with this chart. Develop it fully. Memorize it. Internalize it. Be ready to personalize it when the real bell rings in a competitive battle. It will definitely give you a smile in your stomach and raise your confidence, passion, and speed.

My company's completed answers on differentiation are shown here for your review. They incorporate all three elements of the umbrella: company, solutions, and core values.

Things That We Are Proud of and That Distinguish Us.		What You Can Expect From Us. What We Stand For.
Company	**Solutions**	**Core Values**
1. Boutique firm with consulting and sales training expertise. We don't dump and run. We roll up our sleeves and get the work done.	1. Comprehensive curriculum in competing on value. Know, price, sell, and live.	1. Passion. We have boundless enthusiasm and love for our work. For us, work is fun. We have a fierce desire to help our clients achieve their goals.
2. Deep and narrow strategy within the financial services industry. We are not all things to all people. We can look you in the eye and confidently say, "That's not good enough."	2. Unique and proprietary Value Ladder™ process.	2. Commitment. We have emotional and intellectual commitment to organizational and personal growth. We bring a mindset of innovative learning and dedication to all our client relationships.
3. Global best of breed in helping organizations and financial professionals discover, articulate, and capitalize on their unique value. (Ask our clients.)	3. Transform leadership teams and reinvigorate the spirit of firms and individuals. We build culture.	3. Trust. We earn this coveted distinction due to our clients' total confidence in our abilities, integrity, and character. Our clients are confident in us because of our faith in our work and ourselves. We always do what is right for our clients.
4. PriceMetrix Strategic Partnership. We have unique perspectives on helping professionals realize their value.	4. Raise levels of confidence, passion, and speed. No more winging it!	4. Respect. We treat our clients, and each other, with the utmost respect. We regard each client relationship as a special privilege. We are constantly considerate and appreciative and always strive to exceed our clients' expectations.
5. Team. Knowledge of the financial services industry, experiences, and insight. We're a tough act to follow.	5. Extensive list of client successes within the financial services industry: • We get it. • We change people's lives. • We provide real value. • We help people win.	5. Value. We are unique because we know our value and constantly strive to understand what our clients value. We also believe that value is not only the operative word in business today but the single most compelling word that must be in financial professionals' vocabularies. We are experts at helping organizations compete effectively using the philosophies of value.

How would you fill in this chart for your firm? Are you up for the challenge? Are you winging it? See for yourself. Better yet, ask some other members of your firm to fill it out and then compare answers. Once you complete the process, you'll get great satisfaction in one of two ways: you or your firm will take your ability to distinguish yourself to levels you may only have dreamed about or you've got some work to do. Why wouldn't you want to know where you stand?

Open your umbrella or your virtual file cabinet when you need it. If you're like me, if your day or meeting suddenly turns rainy, you'll feel better just knowing it's there.

Strategic Questions to Consider

- Who are your real competitors? Which ones do you typically run up against?
- Which competitors should you be able to speak about knowledgeably and proficiently?
- Do you get excited when you think about the solutions you provide your clients?
- Can your team properly differentiate your business and solutions from key competitors?
- Does your firm have specific values by which it abides?
- Do you have individual values by which you abide?

Final Thoughts

Asking what makes you different is a natural question for anyone with options to choose.

If that's the case, be absolutely on target with your response. Get the smile in your stomach. Go to your completed differentiation 3x5 chart and impress someone with your knowledge and skill set.

Remember the umbrella of distinction.

Use it when you need it. Be an expert in first discussing your own firm, your solutions, and yourself.

Knowing your competition is a real competitive advantage.

You impress prospects or clients when you are conversationally proficient. You will feel like you have your act together, and trust me, based on over 30 years of experience, others will feel it, too.

Be strategic. Go to school on key differentiation terms.

Identify key concepts you and your firm should understand, such as uniqueness, competitive advantages, and parity. Speak the language that many of your sophisticated clients would understand.

Do I hear a drum roll here? We're ready to climb the last step of the Value Ladder™, which is "Why should I do business with you?"

What's your real value?

Why Should I Do Business With You? (Real Value) 9

We've climbed a long way up the Value Ladder™. Can you recall climbing something else and reaching the top? Do you remember that feeling of exhilaration, knowing you had achieved your goal?

Understanding the concept of real value is a great way to end the climb up the Value Ladder™. You should now be ready to think and talk about the real value that you provide to clients. That will enable you to answer the last critical question on the Value Ladder™, which is "Why should I do business with you?"

Value Versus Real Value

Let's review the concept of value again and how it changes when you put the word *real* in front of it. How is value, as used in our Unique Value Proposition™ (UVP™), different from real value?

You define value in your UVP™ as how well your solutions help achieve your clients' goals. Remember, it's the proposition of what you do uniquely well. In essence, it tells someone, "Here's what I could do for you." It conveys a professional attitude and that, yes, you are unique. It's delivered with confidence, passion, and speed.

If someone asks me what my value is, I say, "I help financial professionals go through a process to discover, articulate, and capitalize on their unique value." But what is the real value of my work? It is the application of my expertise, specialization, and core competencies for my clients. It represents the results, both qualitative and quantitative, that they can achieve by working with me.

Clients' main concern is real value. Think of the most pressing issues on someone's desk. If you can help him or her address those issues, tackle the problems that haunt him or her, and set him or her on a path to meeting his or her most cherished goals, that's real value.

Here's a simple example. Take the cap off a felt-tip marker. The cap is a feature. The benefit is that it helps keep the marker from drying out. What's the real value, though? Well, if the marker doesn't dry up, then it lasts longer and you won't have to buy another one as quickly. It will keep your costs down and save you money. Immediately, you can see that the benefit—keeping the marker from drying out—is significant. When you talk to clients, make sure they see how the benefits of working with you will translate into desirable outcomes for them. That's when they will be able to see the real value.

A subtle difference exists between value and real value, but the difference is extremely significant. Again, real value is the actual application to the real world. It's not your claim of value or something implied. It's explicit. You can prove it. You've done it for others. Prospects can talk to your existing clients, and they will verify and validate this value to the fullest. You know you've provided real value when you have tangible success stories of how you've helped others meet their goals.

I always like to ask my prospective clients, "How will you measure my success?" Then I zip my lips and wait for their response. It really tells me a lot about their thought process. I want to know the answer so I can assess how they judge me. How can I exceed the prospect's expectations if I don't know what they are? What is it about my UVP™ that caught his or her attention? What is the real value he or she is seeking? How can I make my value come alive to him or her so he or she becomes one of my passionate advocates?

Our business culture today is bottom-line sensitive. Everybody wants to know what they are receiving in return for what they are paying. Earlier, we described the characteristics of the changing client. When it comes to making a decision based on your value, your prospects are probably thinking the following:

- How much money are you going to cost me?
- What will you do for me in return?
- What's in it for me? What benefits will I get out of our relationship? How will those benefits translate to real value?
- You want me to pay you a fee—but for what? Preparing a form that I need or real advice that I can use?

- What is the totality of your value package?
- How will your services align with my goals?
- What's the real value?
- So, tell me again, why should I do business with you?

These questions illustrate why we need to be truly consultative. Strategic questioning is required. You've got to feel as though you are playing chess, not checkers, with your prospect. The game of checkers is transactional because you focus on one step at a time. Chess involves longer term strategy and a series of interrelated steps to meet your goals.

Many CPAs only do what the client asks, such as prepare a tax return. It drives me crazy when people are so short term in their focus. They are only offering the basic services and not really asking, or listening, to the clients' needs, much the way a vendor delivers goods to your door and then moves on. Many clients must go to several financial professionals to get their needs met because each one's service is so shallow and short sighted. But most serious clients have only one consultant: someone who has earned that coveted distinction of trusted business advisor.

The concept of short term versus long term should get you thinking about whether you are perceived as a vendor or partner.

Getting Out of the Vendor Parking Lot

Early in my sales career I remember driving to meetings and sales appointments and parking in my prospect's parking lot. Can you visualize the vendor's spaces in the parking lot? To have some fun (but I was serious), I would ask my clients where the partners park. I would always get a chuckle, but they would get my point: I wanted to be thought of (and treated) as a partner, not a vendor.

If you're positioning real value, acting like a strategic partner and earning the coveted distinction of trust, then you will be parking where the partners park. Another way to evaluate real value is by the impact you actually make on your clients. Let's take a look at another ladder now: the Financial Entrepreneur Impact Ladder™.

The Financial Entrepreneur Impact Ladder™

The Financial Entrepreneur Impact Ladder™ depicts five different levels of working with a client. They start at the lowest level and move upward and are as follows:

1. *The friendly pest.* This is the individual who was "in the neighborhood" and decided to stop by to say hello and see how you are doing. He or she wastes time and accomplishes very little.

   Do you hand out brochures and promotional materials to clients (got any golf balls)? So does this person! It's a nice gesture, but in the end, you are really competing on value, not handouts. Don't be a professional visitor; bring something of value when you arrive.

2. *The price cutter (aka the price advisor).* Have you ever competed on price before? Have you ever been challenged by a prospect to cut your fee to meet a competitor's pricing proposal? "What, Mr. P.? My competitor said they would charge you how much? Sure, I can beat that fee." Have you ever said those words? This has become a much bigger concern in the last few years, as fee pressures and price competition have mounted.

Competing on a price is a tough road to take, however, because there will always be someone who can beat your price. In the end, rock bottom fees are not the kind of value that will retain good clients.

3. *The technical presenter.* You'll find yourself still parking in vendor parking lots if a lot of your time is spent as a technical presenter. This behavior is easy to spot when you are watching someone else in action. Who is doing all the talking? Not you, if you're smart. You should be listening twice as much as talking, but the technical presenter dominates the conversation.

   When talking to clients or prospects, technical presenters also often use jargon familiar only to themselves. Some like to show off their knowledge of the Internal Revenue Code or arcane Financial Accounting Standards Board pronouncements. You usually get a friendly but puzzled look from your prospects unless they are technically trained, as well. If this describes you, you need to follow these adages:

   a. Try to understand before you are understood.

   b. Be impressed before you become impressive.

   c. Be interested before you become interesting.

   d. Listen before you are listened to.

   Get the picture?

   If you're at this stage, please, enough already with the mystery language. Slow down. Connect emotionally and logically with your prospect. Don't overwhelm him or her with your mind. Let him or her overwhelm you with his or her long term goals.

   Have you ever been a technical presenter?

4. *The need satisfier.* Finally, you're starting to move into that coveted partner area. As the title implies, you are entering a stage where you can start satisfying needs. The following behaviors define the need satisfier:

   a. You realize why you have two ears and one mouth.

   b. You are getting better at listening and responding to needs but can still improve.

   c. You are hearing potential opportunities that require further clarification and could represent needs you can meet.

   d. You appreciate the basics of consulting dialogue.

   e. You usually ask good questions.

f.   You position the features and benefits of your products and services in a way that clients understand.

g.   You know how to recognize your clients' emotions and attitudes, and you can answer most of their questions.

h.   You meet with clients or prospects in person, and you are beginning to understand how to make a connection with them, respectfully and confidently.

i.   You know how to close the deal and request commitments.

j.   You know how to play checkers (transactional mode) and are learning how to play chess (strategic and highly consultative).

5.   *The strategic partner.* No more vendor parking lots at this level. You are inner circle quality. Your client appreciates your value, pays you for it, and passionately recommends you to others. This advocate wants to help you because of the help you have given him or her. The core behaviors of a world-class financial professional who is viewed as a high level strategic partner are as follows:

   a.   *Thinks and acts as an entrepreneur.* You continually invest time and effort in steps that will distinguish your organization, your team, and yourself.

   b.   *Realizes that the most important thing they have to sell is themselves.* You know how to position the value that you and your firm provide through your solutions. You realize that the client is making the connection with you or your team and that you are an expert.

   c.   *Competes on value.* You know it, you can price it, you can market it, and you actually live it.

   d.   *Truly exhibits consultative behaviors.* Your attitude, knowledge, skills, and tools are professional and ready to be put to use.

   e.   *Earns the coveted distinction of trust.* Trust is defined as the total confidence that others have in three things you possess: integrity, character, and abilities. How many of your clients truly trust you?

   f.   *Thinks and acts like a partner.* You sit on the same side of the table with your client.

   g.   *Exhibits respect in conversation.* You clarify, confirm, and are masterful at acknowledging your clients' thoughts and statements (that is, you make the emotional connection).

h. *Can illustrate a process.* You have a unique, comprehensive client relationship process, one that further distinguishes you.

i. *Demonstrates solid confidence.* Current and potential clients can sense it. They recognize that you are a true professional who deserves their trust.

j. *Passionate in all that they do and say.* You love what you do and it shows.

k. *No hesitation in response to critical questions.* You're ready for anything the client might throw at you, and your answers demonstrate respect and forethought.

So, how would your clients rate you on this ladder of behaviors?

The Qualitative and Quantitative

Now that you have a better sense of value versus real value, and of the behaviors of a strategic partner, let's imagine that you're deep into a dialogue with a potential client. If you win this business, it literally could make your year. Up to this point, you've done everything right. You've laid out a careful strategy, and it's working. Just when you think you're at the end of this process and you're getting near closure, the prospect looks at you and says in a nice, but challenging, way, "So, why don't you net it out for me. Why should I do business with you?"

When you hear those words, what are you thinking? Where does your mind go? How do you feel? More often than not, this question helps the prospect put the final dot on the exclamation point and is meant to challenge, even if a challenging tone is not used. This is a good time to reinforce everything you've been sharing with the prospect throughout the Value Ladder™ process. Do you feel you are ready to sum everything up and that you will be confident in your delivery?

A client can ask the same question in many ways. Your prospect could say something like, "I'm not sure I have enough information to make a decision right now." There may still be some skepticism on his or her part. Maybe you haven't really connected yet. Or it might be a genuine stall on his or her part. Maybe the prospect is still evaluating other alternatives and is having a tough time making a decision.

But remember (and how could you forget by now?), business is first a meeting of the hearts and then it becomes a meeting of the minds. When you have emotionally and logically connected with your prospects, you have achieved the ultimate alignment of your value to theirs. It's important to understand that real value is achieved by qualitative means and measured by quantitative means.

An example of a qualitative value is helping someone find his or her peace of mind. Maybe you're in an estate planning dialogue with the potential client and you're discussing his or her legacy. Maybe there are charitable giving issues, a desire to make a difference, or some other intrinsic values that are important to that prospect. Perhaps a small business owner wants to improve his or her quality of life or find an easier way to run a business whose day-to-day workings have become too cumbersome and tedious. Or you may be talking to a client who knows that he or she needs an audit, but you know that what he or she really wants is to purchase a new facility that will help him or her expand production and revenues.

Quantitative value refers to a logical connection—mind to mind. Your prospect may want to grow the business and asks you how to do it. You develop a plan to help him or her position the company to expand sales or make strategic acquisitions. You work together to achieve the goal. That's quantitative value.

Often, the achievement of quantitative value may make it possible for the individual to achieve what's in his or her heart. The business grows, so the company owner can finance the expansion of which he or she has always dreamed. On the other hand, you might have dialogues with prospects on qualitative issues first (heart to heart), then map out a plan to achieve the quantitative, or logical, goals (mind to mind). A company founder wants to pass the company on to the next generation, so you put together a business plan that will help make that possible. No matter how the effort begins, in the end, you're delivering real value.

Take a look at the following list of quantitative and qualitative value attributes. You can surely come up with many more based on what you do in your practice every day, but this will help get you thinking about how to provide more real value to your own prospects and clients.

Qualitative

- Leave an inheritance for children or a favorite cause
- Make a difference in the community
- Support charitable endeavors
- Enhance quality of life

- Make it more enjoyable and less stressful to run a business
- Expand confidence
- Have more time for myself

Quantitative

- Increase assets
- Boost revenues
- Streamline operations
- Accelerate cash flow
- Protect assets
- Reduce risk
- Lower costs

What's the Bottom Line?

You've come to the point where the potential client wants a summary of your presentation, a concise reason why he or she should do business with you. This is your chance to connect your unique value back to him or her, based on what he or she has shared with you.

The tangible examples of successes you've had with other clients will help you here. This, added to what you have learned from your current prospects, should tell your potential client without a doubt how you can help achieve his or her goals. A dialogue may sound like this:

Challenging Prospect (Mr. and Mrs. P.): "You've presented a compelling case for consideration. One final question: why should we do business with you?"

(Big gulp) You lean back in your chair, possibly tempted to wing it. Time out. Rewind. That was the person you were before you started reading this book.

Now, you are in a relaxed position. A smile begins in your stomach. You sit up with self-assurance. You feel you have exemplary confidence, passion, and speed. The new and improved CPA's response might sound like this:

CPA (long version): "Thank you, Mr. and Mrs. P. I appreciate your interest and the possibility to partner with you. It would be a privilege to have you both as clients and I truly value the opportunity." (That's an emotional connection.) You continue, "We've discussed your key long term financial planning goals. You have major issues to contend with in the broad areas of tax and estate planning, retirement, and income protection. You also are concerned about providing for the needs of both your children and your parents.

"Earlier, I presented my firm's UVP™ to you. That was our proposal of value. We're experts in what you are seeking. You should now have a sense of our business beliefs and, most important, the process we will employ going forward to meet your goals. We've also shared some of the successes we've had with clients with similar goals, showing you how we've helped them achieve their goals. Hopefully, you are comfortable with how we've differentiated our firm, solutions, and team.

"The real value will be in the results we'll be able to produce for you. As we've done for others, we can save you money and put a plan into action to help you increase the certainty of achieving your long term goals.

"Once again, we value the opportunity to strategically partner with you. May we begin that partnership now?"

– OR –

CPA (short version): "Because we can provide real value to you, we can help you achieve your goals. We've demonstrated it for others, and we can do it for you. But you need to be comfortable with what we bring to the table—our value and how it aligns with what you've shared with us. We have the expertise and the specialization you are seeking."

That short example could be adapted for a large manufacturer seeking an audit or an individual with tax concerns. In either case, the reality is that you can't talk like this unless you genuinely know what you're doing, have demonstrated your value to others, and have helped others achieve their goals. Then, your value becomes real.

Jumping the Gun

Are you wondering if the question, "Why should I do business with you?" will come up early in the dialogue, before you've been able to answer the other six critical questions? My experience shows that it usually does not. Think about this. Why should a client ask why he or she should do business with you if he or she never got around to asking what you do?

If it does come up early in the dialogue, I might say something like, "Well, there are many reasons why I believe you should hire me, but first, it's important that I have a good understanding of what you are looking for and what you value. Then, I can tell you if I am capable of providing it in line with what you are seeking in a strategic partner."

Answering this question prematurely would be like a doctor prescribing a medication for an illness before he even runs tests and determines a diagnosis. It's too soon to make that call.

Making the Connection

When your work is accepted and applied and your clients accomplish goals because your value meets their needs, then it all becomes real to them. If not, then you're just making claims that sound good but don't really register with the client. When I used to teach how to handle potential client skepticism during my early days at the former Xerox Learning Systems, I explained that skepticism is simply doubt: prospects doubt your ability or services. Some of your potential clients also may have doubts, but you, the consummate CPA, can't have any doubts. Any organization, team, or individual must show examples of real value. Remember, real value is not the same as your UVP™. Real value is the application of your unique value in a customized way to prospective clients. It's showing that you can and have provided results. Another key word to remember is *impact*. Think about the impact that your work has made on your clients' lives and businesses.

The UVP™ tells our prospects and clients what we do, but the UVP™ must be applied in the real world. When you develop custom services for your clients, you suddenly realize you are creating AHAs for yourself and your clients. Begin with your own AHAs. How can you expect someone else to connect with you if you don't feel this way inside yourself? That's your inner glow. If this isn't beaming out of your heart and soul, how do you really expect to make that connection emotionally and logically with someone else? How can he or she feel it if you don't feel it?

When you recognize that you provide value and that you can bring your proposal of value alive for prospects in a way that will help them achieve their big picture goals, then it becomes real. That, in essence, is the big AHA for your clients.

Strategic Questions to Consider

- How do you usually respond to the seventh Value Ladder™ question, which is, why should I do business with you?
- How does your team respond?
- How do you define the real value you provide to your clients?
- Have you ever asked if they are aware of your real value?
- How would your clients define the real value you provide?
- Do you consistently ask your clients how they will measure your success?
- Are you currently measuring the real value you offer?
- How are you documenting your real value?

Understanding your real value is key. This is an important concept for you to master. It requires continued introspection, quality dialogue with your existing clients, and asking for honest feedback on the value you've provided.

Questioning your existing clients will give you greater understanding. You'll learn about areas you can improve to ensure you are on the path to providing real value. If you are providing real value, you increase the certainty of establishing a client for a lifetime. These are clients who you covet and clients whose values are understood and who appreciate and accept your real value and share them with future prospects. Isn't that what we all want?

Case closed.

Final Thoughts

This final question should be the easiest to answer.

Why? Because if you've got the previous six answers down, this one merely sums it all up.

Think impact and results.

Do your best to connect your work to what's most important to your clients. Help them achieve their goals, and you'll have a client for life.

Look me in the eyes and net it out.

That's right. Be confident. Let me feel your passion. Show me there is no winging it in this response.

Touch my heart. Get in my head.

My uncle, John, a 50-year member of the insurance industry, told me he was taught that your heart is a lot closer to your head than your wallet. Worry about the heart and mind; everything else will take care of itself.

Now that you've climbed to the top rung of the Value Ladder™, do you see the value, both in the journey you've made and in yourself and what you do for clients?

Congratulations!

Let's review the Value Ladder™.

The Value Ladder™ in Review 10

The climb up the Value Ladder™ certainly has been high and far. By now, you've learned a lot through the Value Ladder™ process. Before we address advanced applications, cultural issues, and creating a value strategy, let's revisit some key points:

- The value revolution is alive and well. Clients are changing, have greater options, and are demanding custom solutions.
- Many professional services have become commoditized.
- First impressions happen only once, so improving your answers to client questions will help make a good first impression.
- The Value Ladder™ process can help you compete on value.

Here's where you stand after reading this far in this book:

- You should have a better understanding of how to introduce yourself, your team, or your firm.
- You have learned techniques for introspection and the creation of your Unique Value Proposition™ (UVP™).
- You can identify your core business beliefs and philosophies regarding the solutions that you present to others.
- You can define your unique process, an important way to distinguish yourself, by how you partner with clients to achieve their goals.
- You can analyze your client base and consider client retention and growth over a lifetime and understand its value to you.
- You can share client successes and solutions you have provided without betraying client confidentiality.
- You can differentiate yourself from the competition in three ways: through your organization; your solutions; and, most important, yourself.

- You understand real value and how to measure it qualitatively and quantitatively.
- You can use your virtual file cabinet instinctively and in the moment. It is a compelling seven drawer cabinet that can be opened and closed anytime.
- You can improve your ability to deliver your message with confidence, passion, and speed—with no more winging it.

The Value Ladder™ is the chassis on which you will build your personal or organizational message of value. It's the cornerstone, albeit seven separate stones. It starts off as seven separate questions, but as you continue to climb up the Value Ladder™, those seven separate questions should eventually become a chain—a value chain.

Is your personal or organizational message tight and connected, like a great, effortless golf or baseball swing? Or is it disjointed, with pieces all over the place and everybody telling the firm's story in their own way? That's the power of properly completing the Value Ladder™. You develop this unbelievably tight message and all parts of your story are integrated and seamlessly connected. The value chain evolves, and you really start to feel it coming together with a lot of hard work and practice. Don't you think that's something worth achieving?

Let's also revisit some key instructional design issues regarding the development of the Value Ladder™:

1.   The power of the model is in its simplicity. It's an easy model to understand and follow; it flows logically. It's not an easy process, however. When you try to answer questions about yourself and your value, believe me, it's tough. Emotions are high, and frustration and confusion often arise. Exhaustion can set in as you try to figure things out. When it's a challenge to answer questions, I usually have some fun and say aloud, "Welcome to discovering your value." It's not supposed to be easy, but the positive outcomes are enormous. Exhilaration leads to high fives, which lead to

individuals experiencing AHA moments, which leads to the development of confidence, passion, and speed—slowly but surely.

I teach it in a linear fashion. We start at the bottom and work our way up. This is done for a reason. Many clients do, in fact, ask questions in this order. If they don't, they are no doubt thinking about these questions in one form or another.

The additional power of the model is that it allows you to capture all the key critical questions in a compelling, thoughtful way that will further prepare you to distinguish the most important thing you have to offer—you.

2. The Value Ladder™ is flexible. The real world dictates that you must be in the moment. You need not only be prepared but also adaptable and fluid, as well, realizing you may need to open a virtual file cabinet drawer at any point throughout your dialogues with prospects. Be prepared for the unexpected.

For example, you are in a meeting with a prospect and she jumps right into asking questions about your process immediately after you've answered the first question, who are you. In other words, your prospect has leaped from question one to question four on the Value Ladder™. Don't feel handcuffed. You can't say, "Well, that's a good question, but I need to tell you more about who I am, what I do, and why I do it, and then I'll be happy to answer how I do it."

Instead, you must realize that in answering Value Ladder™ questions, you can go from step one to step seven to step four to step two. You can go all over the map. Usually, though, the questions that prospects will ask follow a logical sequence, and then, the answers just flow naturally.

Even if the prospect poses questions out of order, be sure to be specific in answering each Value Ladder™ question he or she might ask. Stay on that rung of the Value Ladder™ with the prospect for a minute. You will demonstrate respect and improve your ability to connect emotionally. Your intuition will tell you where to move next.

The Value Ladder™ will help you stay in control. This is not a mechanical process; you should be flexible, as well. When you start feeling that smile in your stomach, you're there.

3.   The Value Ladder™ was built for a total consultative approach. Clients seeking new options often have two separate agendas. One side of them says, "Do you really know what I value? Ask me questions, listen intently to me, be respectful, and find out what's important to me." However, be prepared because another side of them is asking how your value aligns with what they value.

When you become proficient in answering these questions, you'll find that the confidence you express and your ability to pull information out of your virtual file cabinet will take you to deeper levels of dialogue that you may never have otherwise reached. You will easily be able to address both client agendas.

4.   Although the Value Ladder™ is taught in a linear fashion, your final answers are best developed when you use your virtual screwdriver and tighten up previous steps after you learn a new one.

When my father taught me to change a tire, he showed me how to tighten each lug nut slowly to support the wheel and then to go back and make sure each lug nut was on tight enough. The same principal applies to the Value Ladder™. You should work on your UVP™, then go back and tighten your background screws a little more. Then, after you work on your business beliefs, come back and tighten your UVP™ and background screws. Repeat the process as you continue your climb.

Your Value Ladder™ answers will get tighter and tighter. They'll fit so well that, like a good set of tires that are in total balance, they'll move you forward with the compelling story of your business—tight, in balance, and providing a world-class ride for your prospects.

5.   Memorize the Value Ladder™. I mean really get it down. Like a good actress or actor memorizing lines, you can play the role in ways you might not have imagined. Athletes and other star performers get their routines down so well that we're wowed by their performances but never fully appreciate the time and effort that go into the quest for excellence.

The best way to memorize the Value Ladder™ was proposed by a participant in a Michigan program. "Who, what, why, how, who, what, why," he offered. I had no idea where he was going with this comment. He explained, "These are the first words of each question going up the Value Ladder™, and it's a great way to remember it and use it." Just start at the bottom with, "Who are you?" and climb up.

Why should I do business with you?

What makes you different?

Who have you done it for?

How do you do what you do?

Why do you do what you do?

What do you do?

Who are you?

Try singing the song "Kumbaya" with those words. Who, what, why, how ... who, what, why. Sing it out as I do with participants. Have some fun learning the process. You'll always remember it.

Beyond memorizing the questions and rationales on the Value Ladder™, eventually you need to memorize your answers. You might at first feel a little mechanical because you're not used to it. I will tell you this, though, through many years of experience: the more you memorize, the easier it is to personalize. It's counterintuitive, but it works.

6. Internalize your responses. Imagine you are preparing for the biggest test of your life. The class you've signed up for is called Discovering Your Value, and your professor will be quizzing you with questions on the most compelling story you'll ever need to provide a prospect or client: the story of you, your business, and the value you provide.

Remember the time and effort you put into some of those high school and college tests? How important was it for you to ace that big exam, to get your average up, and to stand out in the crowd with various distinctions, such as membership in the National Honor Society or graduating magna cum laude or summa cum laude? It takes a lot of time to get to great, so start thinking extraordinary.

In past programs, I've worked with an Olympian, several former professional athletes, a participant in the World Cup, triathletes, Green Berets, and an Army Ranger. I've talked to them about commitment, and I've gotten some passionate responses. Are you that passionate about being your best? How much more can you improve your ability to stand out in the crowd?

7.   Remember to personalize your responses. This is where you begin to further separate yourself from other CPAs in a prospect's pile of business cards. You should have one set of answers for all seven Value Ladder™ questions, but learning how to make them come alive for various people is a real art.

My conversation with a senior executive of a major public accounting firm may start with the executive asking, "So, what do you do, Leo?"

I answer, "We specialize and partner with firms like yours to help your professionals distinguish themselves from your core competitors. We help them keep and grow their existing clients and get more business by truly learning how to compete on the value they provide."

The next meeting is an hour later with a managing partner from a top 100 CPA firm who asks me the same question. I then say, "We specialize and partner with firms like yours to help your CPAs further distinguish themselves from their core competitors. We also can help your partners and professionals go through a process to learn how to distinguish your firm and become a firm of choice. We teach them to further understand how to deliver their value more effectively within their communities, and we train and coach the professionals in their offices to ultimately compete on the value they provide." I talk more about the process here because this firm might be more interested in a complex engagement in which we'll delve deeply into process.

Then, I find myself at the small community CPA firm, now in conference with a group of their partners. They ask, "So what do you do, Leo?"

I respond, "I help committed, dedicated, serious CPAs like yourselves discover your value and teach you how to articulate it with increased confidence, passion, and speed." This time, I tailor my answer to a firm that is more interested in what I can do for the individuals in a smaller practice.

Three different scenarios, but I needed to answer the question regarding my uniqueness on three different levels that speak to listeners with three different types of needs. All of the answers flow out of my one UVP™. You simply need to know how to make your UVP™ come alive to the various people with whom you come in contact.

How would it work in a CPA practice? Let's return once again to the CPA on the golf course who we talked about in chapter 4. We discussed his conversational rendering of his UVP™: "I'm a CPA who works with people like you to address tax and financial planning concerns. My firm has particular expertise and advanced credentials in this area, and we work with clients to identify their financial goals and help them achieve them." We also gave an example of how he would extend the UVP™ to discuss college planning with a potential client. But the basic UVP™ can be personalized for, say, a high net worth individual, someone nearing retirement, an individual with estate planning concerns, or any number of situations. Similarly, we also looked at how an auditor might use the message in the UVP™ to focus on the many ways that the business information found in an audit (or a review or compilation, for that matter) could be used to address a client's goals. Rehearse your conversations for the clients you want, and you will see the words starting to flow.

Just remember to protect the integrity of your UVP™! Find the right way to express your value and stick with it. You'll be amazed at how well it works. Enjoy the climb to greatness.

Communication: An Art and a Science

Many CPAs over the years have told me that managing their firms is both an art and a science. What they're saying, in other words, is that they need to make decisions with both their hearts and heads. You have to communicate to your coveted prospects and clients in the same way.

Imagine that you are a genius who has created the perfect formula for the marketplace. Now, you have to apply your intelligence to communicating the wonder of what you have achieved. Just make sure you apply the creative and artistic touch, both in writing and, more important, when verbalizing, so that you truly stand out from the crowd.

Next, let's analyze some Value Ladder™ applications.

Now is the time to wow your prospects.

Advanced Applications for Your Value Ladder™ 11

In the preface to this book, I told you about a practitioner I know who insists that CPAs are the greatest salespeople out there, or at least they should be, given the value they provide to their clients. Well, if you weren't deeply in touch with your own unique value before you started this book, you certainly should be now! Now that you better understand how to articulate that value, let's put your new understanding to work. In the next three chapters, we'll talk about practical ways to apply the Value Ladder™, integrate it into your firm culture, and use it to make key strategic decisions. Let's get started talking about practical applications.

Getting to Real Value

Given all you've learned, the challenge now is applying your new skills to the real world. To reach its highest level of validation, this application must achieve results. In your case, it might be new clients or more engagements for existing clients.

Sound familiar? Sound like real value? You have to be able to apply the theory in order to achieve results. Remember your Unique Value Proposition™ (UVP™), your proposition of value? Remember your effort to find your real value? Now's the time to apply your UVP™ to achieve those goals, both qualitative and quantitative.

Numerous applications make your Value Ladder™ come alive. We will talk about six specific examples and illustrate unique applications to give you a greater sense of the flexibility of the entire model. Remember, the power of the model is in its simplicity. It's an easy model to understand and follow, and it flows logically. Also, don't forget that this model is always used consultatively, with professional respect. You should always seek first to understand then strive to be understood. Ask a lot of questions. Really get to know your prospects. Remember the two-ears-one-mouth theory. There will be a logical point for you to open your file drawers. Intuition should alert you. The first two applications that follow will give you a take-charge model for those prospects who would be more comfortable hearing about you first before they start opening up about themselves. Sometimes, sales opportunities go this way. Prospects may want to warm up to you as the first step on the road to earning their trust.

The First Application: The Value Ladder™ Comes to Life

The following client dialogue illustrates how to use the steps of the Value Ladder™ effectively. This is a long version, but it can be used confidently with a prospect.

"Mr. P., I'd really like to thank you for seeing me today, and I'd like to make the best use of the time you've allotted for our meeting. After reviewing your objectives, I have developed an agenda and some core, critical questions to discuss. I would first like to further review with you who I am, properly introduce my organization to you, and provide some professional and personal background to give you a better perspective.

"The second area that I would like to focus on, Mr. P., is what we do. We've developed a compelling UVP™. It's a statement that will tell you our core services and what value we propose to deliver. I'll net it out for you.

"Third, I'd like to tell you why we do what we do. Our firm has five core business beliefs. I'd like to spend some time with you to review them. They are very important because they really describe what drives our thinking today.

"The fourth area, Mr. P., is how I work with clients like you. We have a very comprehensive five step process, and I'll be happy to illustrate this process for you.

"The fifth step in my presentation will give you a better sense of who we have done this for. We've had tremendous client success, and because I specialize in working with individuals like yourself, I'd like to share with you some of my clients' broader issues and how we've been able to align our unique value to their needs.

"The sixth step is what really makes us different. Mr. P., my clients want to know how our organization and solutions are different. I truly believe that the most important business decision you will ever make is whether you want to sit on the same side of the table with my team and me. I am prepared to talk more about what we stand for individually and what you should expect from partnering with us.

"Last of all, Mr. P., and perhaps the most important question you may want answered, is why you should consider doing business with us. What's the real value we provide? What do we bring to the table, and how does that help you achieve your goals?

"I am prepared to walk you through this process. Is this in line with the expectations you have for the time we'll be spending together today? Are there any other issues of which I should be aware?"

The Second Application: A Shorter Dialogue

You know how flexible the Value Ladder™ can be in any client or prospect situation. Let's say you have limited time in your prospect's office. You want to give the best impression and hit all the points on the Value Ladder™ in whatever time you have. In that case, the following dialogue is concise and gets your message across succinctly and confidently.

"Mr. P., I really appreciate your time today. To make the best use of the half hour you've given me, I'd like to spend a little time sharing with you who I am, explaining my unique value, and outlining my five business beliefs. These beliefs are supported by a very comprehensive five step process. I believe what I offer is uniquely suited to meeting your needs. I've spent a lot of time on this, and I truly believe every step is unique. I'd like to walk you through it.

"I'd also like to share with you a little bit about the clients with whom we work. You are precisely the kind of client we serve, and I'll give you some examples of our successes. I'll spend some time distinguishing my firm and services and explaining why you should consider partnering with my team and me. I'd like you to understand the real value behind what we do and how we can use our expertise to help you accomplish your goals. Now, is that in line with your expectations for our time today? Is there anything else to which I should be sensitive?"

Third Application: Using the Value Ladder™ to Add the Right Services

The Value Ladder™ comes alive even further when you start applying your strategic and consultative questioning skills along with the proper emotional connection skills. In your questioning process, you will be able to turn to areas (or folders) in your virtual file cabinet that connect to whomever you may talk.

For example, a prospect might say, "I need financial statements for my bankers, but I don't need anyone to tell me how to run my business."

You might respond, "Well, Mr. P., tell me more about that. Have you had a bad experience with another consultant or is piloting your own ship part of your business philosophy?" Go deeper in your questioning. Acknowledge the client's agenda or attitude. Clarify. Confirm.

Most CPAs might not ask a prospect a question quite like that. Instead, they may say, "You're right, and I can deliver whatever you want." But if you wanted to take a different tack, you could go into your third file drawer and pull out one of your business beliefs. One example we mentioned earlier is that most business owners suffer too long before asking for professional help as their finances become more complex with growth.

So you would then say, "Mr. P., I understand your desire to run your own shop, but one of our core business beliefs is that great business people often wait too long before getting the kind of professional consulting help that can maximize their profitability and growth potential. This is something I've learned in my years as a professional." You've acknowledged the prospect's attitude but you've shared one of the core beliefs you've picked up as a veteran business consultant. You've also offered an intriguing glimpse into what the prospect might be missing by passing up the small business expertise and value added services that make you unique: greater profits and growth.

Unfortunately, some CPAs throw all of their products, services, and features against the wall and hope something sticks. They "spray and pray." They are not even thinking clearly about positioning their seamless, integrated solutions. Or they "tell versus sell," just like the technical presenter on our impact ladder who does all the talking. If you find yourself slipping into this mode, remember that you should be consulting and asking the critical questions and responding and linking the conversation back to your unique message on the Value Ladder™.

As a result of your world-class listening skills, your prospect should now open up. Look for opportunities to pull manila folders out of your virtual file cabinet. Use them wisely. After all, they should contain everything you need to answer any Value Ladder™ question.

Fourth Application: The Value Ladder™ Questioning Model

Another creative application for the Value Ladder™ is to use it in reverse as a way to probe your clients for information. For example, if you are meeting with a big prospect (for instance, a business owner or corporate executive), you might open by saying, "Thank you for taking the time to talk to me today. Last week, on the phone, you mentioned you had some questions for me, and I'm prepared to answer them. One of the most comprehensive processes I use helps explain who I am, what I do, why I do it, how I partner with people like you, who else I work with, and what makes me different. It also includes why you might want to consider working with me.

"At the same time, I'd like to ask you a few questions, as well, Mr. P. I'd like to know more about you and your background." (This sounds like Value Ladder™ question number one in reverse, doesn't it?)

"I'd also like to know more about the value you provide to some of your own customers or clients in your business, Mr. P." (Hmmm, sounds like Value Ladder™ question number two.)

"What are your core business beliefs today?" (Gee, that's just like Value Ladder™ question number three.) "Can you tell me about the process you use to partner with your most important customers?" (That's a version of Value Ladder™ question number four.)

"And, Mr. P., who might be some of your typical customers? Give me a better sense of the individuals you work with so I can understand your organization better. This helps me better position my work." (That's Value Ladder™ question number five.)

"Can you please tell me how you distinguish your company from your core competitors? How do you separate yourself from the crowd in your industry?" (Sounds like Value Ladder™ question number six.)

"Finally, in your business, what is the real value you provide to your clients, Mr. P.?" (We've reached the top of the Value Ladder™ now.)

See how powerful this application can be? Few of your competitors have likely taken such a comprehensive approach in getting to know the client. Just remember to be conversational and respectful in your approach. Don't ask questions in rapid-fire succession. Take your time, slow down, and you will be surprised at what you will discover. Prospects will be impressed with the professionalism of this approach and the thoroughness of the questions.

Fifth Application: Use the First Three Questions to Determine Compatibility

When you look at the first three questions of the Value Ladder™, you'll see how powerful they really are. They provide a great method for understanding your prospect's background and unique value to others and determining what type of CPA that prospect is looking for. This is when you identify how good a match you are.

You could spend your entire first meeting with a prospect on these three questions. If there is a disconnect with a prospect at this point on the Value Ladder™, most likely, incompatibility will force you to move on to the next prospect.

Often, the first meeting is one of mutual interviewing. If you sense compatibility based on the answers to the first three questions, then you have a solid reason to set up a second meeting where you can go deeper into your process and answer other higher Value Ladder™ questions.

Sixth Application: Competitive Evaluation Tool for High Level Prospects

Turn the Value Ladder™ over to your prospect! That's right, I'm recommending that you share the Value Ladder™ questions with the prospect and suggest that he or she use them in meetings with other CPAs. The answers can help the prospect to distinguish your value from your competition's.

Let's say you're at the point in your discussions when you ask the prospect where you stand and who else they are evaluating. He or she says, "I'm talking to another CPA from a large, reputable firm."

You might respond, "That's great. Help me understand your situation better. How are you going to make your decision, and which criteria will you use?"

If you know for certain that the competition is tough, this may be the time to turn over the Value Ladder™ questions. You may see the risks, but I think it shows unbelievable confidence. Say to your prospect, "Maybe I can add more value to your decision process. Here are seven very powerful questions, Mr. P. You might like to ask them of the other firm or CPA you are interviewing."

Then tell your prospect, "If I were in your shoes, having to make an important decision like this, these are the seven questions I would ask in order to make my choice. You should receive nothing less than black belt answers because you are making a big decision for your future. If you haven't asked these questions, you need to, Mr. P. You need to respectfully challenge us (CPAs) because we should enhance your comfort level with our value before we earn the right to partner with you. This way, you are better informed and can make the best possible decision."

This is a powerful approach. As the CPA, not only will you be asking the right questions, you will be helping your prospect ask them of the competition. Your prospect hasn't even hired you yet and you are already assisting him or her in making important decisions.

A word of caution: you shouldn't try this approach unless you have your own outstanding answers down pat and can deliver them with confidence, passion, and speed. If you're going to be measured against the competition's answers, your own better be good, if not great to extraordinary!

Strategic Questions

- How do you make your value proposition come to life for clients?
- How would you adapt your presentation in different situations?
- How could you use Value Ladder™ questions to learn more about prospects or current clients?

- Should you give the Value Ladder™ questions to potential clients considering another firm? How would you manage that conversation? How should you position your value or your firm's value based on what the prospect learns about the competition?

Final Thoughts

Prepare to be a star.

Rehearse your presentation over and over. Make a conscious effort to really get your story down at a peak level. You can add or subtract from the presentation, depending upon the particular circumstances.

Practice what you preach.

What you've learned through the Value Ladder™ process should give you new confidence. Tap into that confidence in all your business dealings.

Put it to work.

The real value of the Value Ladder™ for you, the CPA, is in using it to make deeper connections with clients; creating better presentations for prospects; and, as a result, maximizing your opportunities.

Don't be afraid to ask clients and prospects the obvious question.

When you learn to deliver your answers to the seven critical questions on the Value Ladder™ with confidence, passion, and speed, you and your message will become so conversationally compelling that your attitude will be, "Why wouldn't you want to do business with me?" When you feel so strongly about what you do, you can say something like this with respect and sincerity. You'll be amazed at the results you will see.

Get ready to develop a culture of value.

Creating a Culture of Value

12

This chapter is for firm leaders who want to develop a culture of value.

The Value Ladder™ can be used by individuals and organizations. As an individual, it's relatively easy to follow through on all that the Value Ladder™ has taught you about yourself and your clients. You set the agenda and call the shots.

Making the most of an organizational Value Ladder™ may be another story. It's one thing to complete an organizational Value Ladder™ but another thing to take responsibility for reinforcing and sustaining it. It's well worth it, however. Seeing behaviors change and, ultimately, hearing new client success stories is truly uplifting, not just to the bottom line but also to organizational spirit and morale. As I've told many clients, it's like a flame or candle that resides within you. You can feel and see the glow becoming more intense.

Beware, though, because I've seen some leaders who just don't get it when it comes to creating a culture of value. Are you one of the following:

- You show up for a meeting, give an eloquent rendition of your vision, display your passion from the podium, and then walk out.
- At an organizational meeting, you take a seat somewhere in the back and tune out what your team or organization is discussing, checking e-mails with your BlackBerry (aka crackberry) or perusing what's in the newspaper.

Are you this person? On a leadership scale of 1–10, with a 10 being the most effective leader driving an organizational culture, how would your firm rank you? How would you honestly rank yourself?

Creating a culture of value begins with an attitude and requires a mighty effort. Your team members have to be united to effect change and achieve the goals that are important to your organization. You can use the Value Ladder™ to promote that unity.

A culture is not only articulated from the top but also practiced at the top. As the managing partner, president, or CEO of your organization (whether a large firm or a small team), you should have completed your Value Ladder™ and everybody—I mean everybody—who is involved with your clients should have completed one, as well.

All team members should be able to demonstrate confidence, passion, and speed. They should understand the value they provide. If you truly believe we are in the midst of a value revolution and that clients are continuing to change, then you must send a consistent message. That means everyone in your organization better know their value and be able to talk about it.

One Message

When I offered training for Fortune 500 companies earlier in my career, the commitments at the organizational level started with the leaders—the CEOs—then trickled down to the vice presidents of sales and marketing; national sales managers; national marketing directors; regional directors; and, finally, right down to the sales force.

Now, consider the organizational structure at the typical CPA firm. What is the difference in their respective marketing methods and messages? Why is one culture easier to create than the other?

Often, CPAs choose their own entrepreneurial way to do business. In some cases, each partner follows his or her own processes and procedures, which makes creating a unified culture very difficult. The partners are busy doing their best for their clients in their own ways, and the firm's positioning and differentiation strategy becomes something they will get to someday, sometime.

How can you counteract this problem? Create one unified, consistent, repeatable message for your marketplace. It's easier to manage and reinforce. Firms should each have a single message that the entire organization espouses. It should proclaim the firm's uniqueness and competitive advantages.

Creating a culture of value should include the seven steps listed subsequently. Like the value chain we depicted in chapter 10, developing this culture also should be a process that ensures everyone is committed to being world class in the delivery or your firm's message. Study the CULTURE list and then conduct your own value audit.

C-U-L-T-U-R-E

Because creating a culture is a top-down approach, let's start at the top and break down the word *culture* letter by letter and analyze it carefully. As your work through the list, use your responses to review the organizational value audit and action plan that you'll find throughout the next few pages. And, of course, the discoveries that you have made on your journey up the Value Ladder™ will help you create thoughtful and insightful answers.

- Challenge yourself and your organization to greatness.
- Understand your value gaps and act.
- Listen aggressively to your clients.
- Total commitment to the initiative.
- Unify your organization.
- Respectful dialogue with all involved.
- Enjoy the ride and measure your success.

Now, let's explore each letter on the culture chain from the top down.

Challenge Yourself and Your Organization to Greatness

We began this book with references to people and organizations that are truly great. Don't you want your clients to put you on that list?

The following questions will challenge you to be sure that the Value Ladder™ answers that you developed are, in fact, helping you become the firm you want to become. Stretch yourself with your thinking. Begin with the end in mind.

- Is your vision so compelling that others in your organization get pumped just listening to you?
- What are you trying to become?
- How do you want to be known?

Creating a culture of value requires living and working hard every day. When you create consistent, memorable experiences, clients will tell others how great you are. The key is to challenge everyone to get involved. You may surprise yourself in the process.

The Organizational Value Audit and Action Plan

1. Challenge Yourself and Your Organization to Greatness

```
|    |    |    |    |    |    |    |    |    |    |
 1    2    3    4    5    6    7    8    9    10
```

NO   SOMEWHAT   TOTAL
COMMITMENT   COMMITTED   COMMITMENT

Specific things we are doing well:

_____
_____
_____

What else could we be doing?

_____
_____
_____

Where are the biggest gaps?

_____
_____
_____

What I will be doing about this. The priorities I will act on:

_____
_____
_____

Understand the Value Gaps and Act

- Are you satisfied with your revenue, clients, overall success, and other aspects of your firm?
- Where do you want to go?
- Do you want to develop a new practice area?
- Do you want to transition to a fee-based practice?
- What are your priorities?
- Where are the gaps?
- What strategies will get you to your goal?
- What tactics do you need to act on?
- Remember all of those qualitative and quantitative examples of real value? What are you striving for?

Start thinking and talking in terms of value goals. What's a value goal? One good example is growth and retention of key clients. Think about estimated lifetime value and use your conclusions to develop an ideal client list. Assess what clients value about you. Are you meeting their needs? Are they aware of all you do for them? Can your team answer these questions? Take steps to grow the relationships you covet then go after more ideal clients.

The Organizational Value Audit and Action Plan

2. Understand Your Value Gaps and Act

| | | | | | | | | | |
|1|2|3|4|5|6|7|8|9|10|

NO COMMITMENT   **SOMEWHAT COMMITTED**   **TOTAL COMMITMENT**

Specific things we are doing well:

_____
_____
_____

What else could we be doing?

_____
_____
_____

Where are the biggest gaps?

_____
_____
_____

What I will be doing about this. The priorities I will act on:

_____
_____
_____

Listen Aggressively to Your Clients

At one business retreat I conducted, one of our exercises was to define *advice*. If it's part of the value you offer clients, then what, exactly, is it?

We identified many attributes of giving advice, but one, in particular, stood out: to listen aggressively. We talked about the word *aggressive*, which, by dictionary definition, is "bold, combative and forceful." It's a passionate word, and listening aggressively would involve paying such close attention to the client's needs that we could offer real value.

Are you truly listening so that you perceive the issues your clients value? Be honest. Do an even better job of acknowledging, clarifying, and confirming. Highly attuned listening skills will differentiate you from the competitors.

The Organizational Value Audit and Action Plan

3. Listen Aggressively to Your Clients

NO COMMITMENT   SOMEWHAT COMMITTED   TOTAL COMMITMENT

Specific things we are doing well:

_____
_____
_____

What else could we be doing?

_____
_____
_____

Where are the biggest gaps?

_____
_____
_____

What I will be doing about this. The priorities I will act on:

_____
_____
_____

Total Commitment to the Initiative

Help your team members by giving them proper training. Set aside some of your budget to educate them on how to compete at top-notch levels based on your firm's unique value.

What else? Value messages should penetrate all communications inside and outside the company. Preach the message. As you would with a good branding strategy, include it on everything. It just makes good business sense.

Finally, live the message yourself. Go through the Value Ladder™ process and use it. Show your team how you put it into action. Communicate with them about the client successes you've achieved with it. Be a role model, and they will emulate you.

The Organizational Value Audit and Action Plan

4. Total Commitment to the Initiative

NO COMMITMENT	SOMEWHAT COMMITTED	TOTAL COMMITMENT

Specific things we are doing well:

_____

_____

_____

What else could we be doing?

_____

_____

_____

Where are the biggest gaps?

_____

_____

_____

What I will be doing about this. The priorities I will act on:

_____

_____

_____

Unify Your Organization

Bring the organization together in the following manner:

1. Memorize, internalize, and learn how to personalize your firm's consistent message for yourself. You will be amazed at how effortless it can become, and you'll be the model that others will try to imitate.

2. Speak from your heart. Let people feel your passion and conviction.

3. Constantly seek out ways to reinforce and sustain the story. Get your marketing team involved. Frame your Unique Value Proposition™ (UVP™) and business beliefs and prominently display them in your office. See how many people start asking you questions about your story and commitment. Be prepared for people to discuss you with unprecedented respect and admiration.

4. Demand participation from your leadership team. Expect great things from your people. Challenge them to get involved, and develop creative ways to help them achieve their goals.

The Organizational Value Audit and Action Plan

5. Utilize All the Requisite Skills

| 1 | 2 | 3 | 4 | 5 | 6 | 7 | 8 | 9 | 10 |

NO
COMMITMENT

SOMEWHAT
COMMITTED

TOTAL
COMMITMENT

Specific things we are doing well:

_____
_____
_____

What else could we be doing?

_____
_____
_____

Where are the biggest gaps?

_____
_____
_____

What I will be doing about this. The priorities I will act on:

_____
_____
_____

Respectful Dialogue With All Involved

People can be respectfully challenged in multiple ways. A meeting of the hearts connotes respect. The important element of a respectful challenge is the tone. You must have the determination of a drill instructor, but if you treat people with respect, you'll always have a willing listener and friend. Don't forget to initiate discussions with staff at all levels about knowing and communicating their value. Involve everyone who comes in contact with your clients. You'll be surprised at what a difference it makes when you enter a strategic dialogue with all members of your team. You will learn. In a business of few guarantees, I can promise you that.

The Organizational Value Audit and Action Plan

6. Respectful Dialogue With All Involved

NO COMMITMENT	SOMEWHAT COMMITTED	TOTAL COMMITMENT

Specific things we are doing well:

_____

_____

_____

What else could we be doing?

_____

_____

_____

Where are the biggest gaps?

_____

_____

_____

What I will be doing about this. The priorities I will act on:

_____

_____

_____

Enjoy the Ride and Measure Your Success

Life is too short not to have fun. Do what you love. Hire team members who love the work, too. Stop worrying. Find your value and articulate it to your ideal clients. They are out there waiting to be helped. Keep a scorecard. Link the program to your most important economic metrics.

The Organizational Value Audit and Action Plan

7. Enjoy the Ride and Measure Your Success

Specific things we are doing well:

_____

_____

_____

What else could we be doing?

_____

_____

_____

Where are the biggest gaps?

_____

_____

_____

What I will be doing about this. The priorities I will act on:

_____

_____

_____

Be Value Ready

The secret to success is not to view competing on value as a quick fix, sales gimmick, or empty slogan. The pacesetting executives know that they must create a culture of value. They understand that before they begin talking about value to clients, value must become a pervasive standard of performance for the entire organization. The savvy leaders are ensuring that their companies are value ready before approaching clients on value terms.

Strategic Questions to Consider

- How can you create a culture of value in your firm?
- Who should be this initiative's champion?
- Is it a commitment that all firm leaders will embrace? If not, how could you bring them all on board?
- Are firm members aware of your firm's unique value? If not, how should they be introduced to it?
- Will your firm develop a UVP™ and business beliefs? How can you include firm leadership and other firm members in the process?
- The answers to many of these questions could involve broad-based efforts. What's the best first step for your firm?

Final Thoughts

Are you truly committed, dedicated, and serious about cultural change?

Don't blow smoke when talking about this. Get in the game completely and watch people want to play with you.

Show up. Be there.

Sit in front and ask questions. Demonstrate your interest. Challenge your leadership team and yourself not to be just great but extraordinary.

No shortcuts, please.

The best companies that I have seen do not cut corners. They look for optimal participation and find a way to get it done.

Now you've worked through the Value Ladder™, thought about how to apply it, and considered the best ways to infuse it into your culture. In the next chapter, we'll help you take what you've learned about the Value Ladder™ and turn it into a one-of-a-kind strategy for your firm. The questions in the next chapter should make you think a little bit differently. Many of them will no doubt be a part of your next offsite strategy meeting.

Competing on Value Begins With a Strategy

13

I have mentioned already that you can use the Value Ladder™ for an individual, team, or organization. Let me tell you a little bit about how my company works with organizations that are getting ready to embark on the Value Ladder™ process. Before we begin a major initiative for a client, we always schedule time with key members of the company's leadership team and appropriate members who interact with the company's clients. We also review critical client data collected from focus groups or surveys. Many times, we pick up the phone ourselves and talk to clients first hand. Why are we doing all this in preparation for Value Ladder™ training?

It is a vital step in preparation for our consultative approach. We refer to this step as the alignment phase in our process. Our alignment phase is all about organizational readiness. Not only does the client need to be ready for some unique introspection, we have to be ready, as well.

The Value Ladder™ is an iterative process. It requires great process facilitation skills to develop a world-class story. You are constantly debating meaning, checking your thesaurus, and wondering if you have the right words in play for each Value Ladder™ step. Participants are constantly searching us out and asking, "Can you take a look at this? Do the words make sense? Does this sound right?"

This step always precedes the development of an organizational Value Ladder™. The same would be the case for specialized practice areas, smaller CPA firms, and sole practitioners. It includes the questions that provide a framework for making the most of what your firm has to offer. They also will help you create a business strategy that sets you apart from the competition, enables you to offer stand-out client service, and ratchets up your firm's success.

When we began the book, I needed to jump start you into the Value Ladder™ process. As we come to the end, I need you to slow down and think about your organizational readiness questions before you start developing your Value Ladder™.

The following pages will definitely make you think. Some questions will jump off the page. You'll probably want to take some of them into your partners' offices immediately and ask them how they would answer the questions. This chapter should challenge you and make you squirm a little as you attempt to make important strategic decisions that can propel your firm forward.

Get your pen and paper ready because you've got some important questions to answer.

Vision

What's your vision for what your firm or practice will look like in the next three to five years?

Consider the following key goals:

1. How many people will your firm employ?
2. What types of clients do you see your firm working with?
3. What types of services will you be offering?
4. What will be your revenue goals?
5. What succession plan issues will you need to consider?

Back in chapter 7, when we talked about who your clients were, we discussed critical emotional issues that can be analyzed for any goal area. Here's a review:

- *Challenges.* Things that inhibit you from achieving your goals.
- *Circumstance.* A situation that accompanies an event.
- *Concerns.* Issues that are of interest or importance.
- *Frustrations.* Situations that leave you disappointed or unfulfilled.
- *Needs.* Things that you want or require.
- *Opportunities.* Situations favorable to the attainment of your goals.
- *Problems.* Questions you raise out of concern or doubt.

Think about these issues when considering these questions:

- Why have you been successful growing at a good pace, even in a changing, challenging environment (assuming you have been growing)?
- When you think of your opportunities, what might limit the growth of your firm? What are your internal and external limitations?
- What are you most proud of having achieved? This question offers some perspective on things close to your heart, as well as insight into how you might be able to differentiate your firm.

What key emotional issues will have an effect on your answers?

In addition, I'd like to know what company outside your profession you would most like to emulate. What qualities or traits of those businesses could be integrated into your firm?

Lastly, in this area, what do your people think about your culture? Remember that employee satisfaction often equals client satisfaction.

Clients

Working with clients allows you to apply your real value. They are the key to the future of your firm and how it will grow and prosper.

I would start your analysis with the following questions:

- Who are your clients? How would you describe them?
- How do you segment them?
- Are their needs continuing to evolve? If so, how?
- What is the current gap between what you offer and what your clients need? (Think also of services and solutions you provide that they don't even know about.)
- What do your clients most appreciate or value about your work?
- Have you lost clients or significant revenue recently? Where are lost clients going?
- What aspects of your value do your clients or the market not fully appreciate? Why?

Services

What is your bread and butter? Are these services commoditized? Is it possible to articulate why your firm offers better service?

These questions merit review and discussion:

- How many different services do you offer clients?
- What are your core services?
- Have you categorized them in a way that makes sense to your team and clients?
- Do partners in different areas work together to sell new services to existing clients?
- What services do you offer that are truly unique (you have exclusivity with these services)?
- In which service areas do you have competitive advantages?
- Given the answers to these questions, are there new services you should add? Are there services you'd like to phase out?

Marketing Strategy

This can be an area of frustration for many firms. This section includes key marketing questions, considers your firm's reputation in your community, and offers some questions to examine your current value proposition. Include these questions in your efforts to improve:

- How do you get clients? What specifically do you do to keep and grow clients?
- What are some of the key elements of your firm's marketing strategy? Which ones work best? Which are less successful?
- What are you doing to help your firm, partners, or associates more effectively market your organization?
- What specific marketing investments have you made to drive new revenues?
- How do you measure the success of your marketing investments?
- What are the untapped opportunities with your own firm (cross selling) or strategic alliance partners?

Reputational Value

In one of my meetings with a managing partner from a top 100 accounting firm, I asked many questions, but one in particular stood out because of the way he responded. I simply asked, "What is your reputational value?"

He immediately said, "That's a great question. Let me think about that." I took it a little further by asking the following questions:

- What do you want others in the community to say about your firm?
- How do you want your clients describing you to others?
- What about your prospects? When you are in a competitive situation, what impression do you want to create?

Another way to look at this is by asking yourself if you are you creating a presence in your absence. Think about that one for a minute. It's a powerful concept. Simply put, even when you're not around, people should have the distinct impression that you have created about your firm; solutions; and, most important, you. Whether you are a top 100 firm or a solo practitioner, your challenge is the same. No need to overthink this. Do people (clients and prospects) like, trust, and value you? Do they consider you their reliable, trusted advisor and tell others about those attributes? Do they, in other words, appreciate your value? Some final questions to consider here are the following:

- What is the reputational value of your firm?
- What do clients and people in the business community actually say about you when you're not around?
- What are you best at?
- What makes your firm great?
- If you have a strategic alliance opportunity, for what area of specialization are you known? (What services or solutions should other CPAs be referring to you?)

If the reputational value of your firm is high, that's a powerful marketing tool. What can you do to enhance your reputational value?

Value Proposition

In putting together your strategy, also review these questions about your value proposition. A key takeaway from this book will be the creation or refinement of your value proposition. You can think of it as answering the fundamental question of life, which is "What do you do?" As we discussed in chapter 4, the underlying answer is not just that you're a CPA but the value that you, as a CPA, provide to your clients. Although reputational value involves perception, your value proposition is the reality that should underline your reputation with clients and the larger business community in the following manner:

- What is the unique value that your firm provides to clients?
- What is the unique value that you individually provide to clients?
- What are your firm's core competencies?
- What is your current value proposition? How would you describe what sets you apart? Is it truly unique?

Financial Metrics

As a business owner myself, I know that managing financial controls is critical. Fee growth is one important benchmark. The years 2005–08 proved to be a great period of fee growth for the accounting profession. How did you fare in comparison? How has your situation changed in recent years? As one managing partner said to me, "Thinking about net income per partner keeps me up at night." Whether you are a solo practitioner or a member of a smaller CPA firm or top 100 firm, consider the following questions to get your financial metrics motor up and running:

- What controls your profitability?
- Which metrics are you keen to keep at current levels?
- Which metrics would you like to see change?
- What are three to five specific ways for you to drive revenue for your firm?
- What is the single most compelling thing you or your firm could do that could dramatically affect the revenue of your firm?
- What changed behaviors will help drive revenues?
- What should you be doing less of to improve profits or revenues?
- What should you stop doing?

Professional Development

This area is near to my heart. So many people just don't understand what it takes to change behaviors.

I'm not concerned here about the mandatory technical training you need or provide to members of your organization; rather, I'm concerned about the marketing skills a professional must have. To kick-start your work in this area, think about the following questions:

- What professional development plans does your firm have?
- How do you train firm members to retain clients and nurture existing client relationships?
- What training do you provide to help your firm members attract new clients?
- Is this training tailored to your firm or profession?
- How much of this is hands-on training given by the rainmakers in your firm that allows staff to use what they learn in real-world situations?

Competition

In chapter 8, we talked about what makes you different. As we mentioned, differentiating yourself involves knowing about the businesses out there that compete against you. You should ask yourself the following questions when you think about how you differentiate yourself from your competitors:

- Who are your competitors?
- Whom do you respect and why?
- How do you fundamentally differentiate your firm from the competition?
- Is there anything that you provide that is truly unique? Something that none of your competitors would offer?
- In what service areas do you have a competitive advantage?

Final Thoughts

Are you warmed up now? How do you put all these insights to work? Here's what I've learned from years of discussions with key leaders and representatives from some of the most prestigious firms around the globe.

Get the right people in the room.

   You want candid feedback from individuals who can help your firm get to the next level. People must speak their mind and tell you the truth and nothing but the truth.

Include your key clients.

   Who better to discuss your value than the people who pay your bills? No one is more qualified to give you the answers you really need to hear.

Use the summary for your strategic planning.

   You'll uncover a lot of information once you start answering these questions. Keep notes then put your findings together into a workable, candid narrative. For example, here's how you might write up the details you learn from the questions in Value Strategy 6 on professional development: "We spend $xxxx each year to send staff to marketing training courses. Most of the courses are specifically for accountants and focus on getting new clients, not on retaining or growing clients. We don't have any in-house training."

Once you put this down on paper, it makes you stop and think. Is this the best strategy for your firm? Is it working, or are you just spending money on skills your people never actually put into practice? Use the summary to develop insights and make decisions that will drive your business plan forward.

Drum roll please!

Off to the final chapter.

Are you ready to act?

What Are You Going to Act On? 14

Here's where you need to take that leap—that risk—and be disciplined and motivated enough to move toward achieving your goals. As I've said throughout the book, it's not an easy process. It's demanding and challenging, which is what great learning and discovery processes are all about. They force you to think.

Dr. David S. Viscott said it best in his book, *Risking: How to Take Chances and Win:* "Before you can act, you must believe you need to change." He spells it out perfectly. "If you cannot take a risk on your own behalf, you are not your own person. You are your biggest problem."

We've talked a lot about going from good to great to extraordinary. To get to your destination, you must act. Before you can act, you must change. You must accept risk. So where do you go from here? Will you be flying, taking a train, renting a car, riding a bike, or taking a leisurely walk? How are you going to move forward?

Many career coaches will tell you that you're either interested or committed. If you are committed to going from good to great, from great to extraordinary, from extraordinary to the best possible person you're capable of becoming, then you must schedule time with yourself to work on the most important thing you present to others—you.

It's like starting the diet, beginning the exercise program or golf lessons, or learning Spanish—it's the coulda woulda shoulda stuff you've always talked about doing. Think about it. You will put yourself through an intensive process of introspection and discovery, thinking in ways you've never thought before. You will push yourself to examine beliefs that you've taken for granted for years. You will realize that this process is very important and you need to act upon it right away.

If you believe that whatever got you to this point is not good enough to get you where you want to go tomorrow, then you must act! Here are some key thoughts on how to get it done. Of course, they assume that you want to act, you're willing to change, and you're ready to take a risk.

The Seven Keys to Successful Action

1. *Work on your personal Value Ladder™*. Just write down your answers. I'm looking for speed here. Maybe your firm already has a brochure that hits some of the points we've discussed, or maybe you're thinking you've just recently gone through a similar process. It doesn't matter. Just start writing. I'm looking for an attitude that's open to improvement. Always, always, always be honest. Are you good, great, or extraordinary? Can you get better? Write on. You can do this on your own, but if you are in charge of a team, remember that it's best if each team member is involved so your ultimate approach and message are consistent.

2. *Schedule retreat time for yourself or your team, or both*. Find some time to truly work on your business. Begin quality dialogue on strategy with yourself or your team. Where are you going? What type of life do you want for yourself and your family? What type of compelling business model will you need to create, fix, or improve to get that life? With the pace of change as fast as it is today, your business plan should be no longer than two years out. There's no harm in developing your dreams for the long term, but be realistic. Continue considering the following strategic questions: Who are your ideal clients? What do you want to be known for? What are you truly great at? What should you be stepping up in the future? Evaluate these questions and answers against your existing Value Ladder™ answers. Your AHAs should continue to happen.

3. *With a better understanding of your business and personal goals, get back to work on your improved Value Ladder™ answers*. Where are the gaps? What do you feel really good about? What needs refinement in your story? Be tough on yourself. If you are leading a team, inspire them to be a part of the process, too.

4. *Get serious about creating a culture of value*. Whether you are a sole practitioner, part of team, or a member of a larger organization, complete the organizational value audit and action plan in chapter 12. This will give a better sense of your current commitment to compete on value and, more important, what should be changed to sharpen that commitment.

5. *Revisit your emotional issues.* Think about your challenges, circumstances, concerns, frustrations, needs, opportunities, and problems. Be honest and introspective. Knowing more about yourself will help you better understand and articulate your value. Once you know your value, you're better able to price and market it. Need I say more?

6. *Visit your clients.* Start with your top 10 ideal clients. Apply aggressive listening techniques. Ask them, "What have we done well? How can we improve? Are there areas in which we haven't been as responsive as you'd like?" Don't ask for referrals now. Don't worry about how your clients can help you at this moment. Just discover everything you can in order to help them more. If you can indeed offer more help, they will give you the best quality referrals without being asked. Reconnecting with your clients will revalidate your value. It also will give you ideas on how to improve your value proposition and delivery of real value. Go for it.

7. *Based on your new and improved Value Ladder™ answers, develop a branding strategy for your marketplace.* From business cards to envelopes and from brochures to Web sites, look for all the ways to proclaim your unique message to potential ideal clients. Assume an attitude of excellence. Whatever you do in your branding strategy, do it within your budget and capabilities. You know that the most compelling story you have to tell is your own, so, craft your strategy, apply your Value Ladder™ insights, and price your value correctly. The easiest thing for you to market should be that competitor in your mirror—you.

A Final Thought to Consider

In light of the rapid changes taking place in the economy and the profession and the challenges that lie ahead for CPAs, competing on value holds tremendous power and potential for you.

I hope this book has been the beginning of your journey to discover your value. You have probably already developed some answers and experienced a few AHAs as you have climbed the seven steps with me.

Stay focused, be a sponge for learning, build your confidence, find your passion, and improve your speed.

Here's one realization I hope you can take away from this book and the Value Ladder™ process: you have a tremendous amount to offer to your clients and everyone else in your professional life. You've been given many gifts, so use them wisely in your life. Enjoy the ride, and as I say to all my friends, "Stay close."

My best,
Leo
P.S.: Oh, by the way, what is your value?

Printed in the United States
By Bookmasters